✝ We Sing and Praise ✝

MUSIC SERIES FOR CATHOLIC SCHOOLS

We Sing and Harmonize

BY

SISTER CECILIA, S.C., M.F.A.

SUPERVISOR OF MUSIC, *Sisters of Charity of Seton Hill*
Greensburg, Pennsylvania

SISTER JOHN JOSEPH, C.S.J., Ph.D.

DIRECTOR OF DEPARTMENT OF MUSIC, *Fontbonne College*
St. Louis, Missouri

SISTER ROSE MARGARET, C.S.J., M.M.

SUPERVISOR OF MUSIC IN ELEMENTARY SCHOOLS
Sisters of Saint Joseph of Carondelet, St. Louis, Missouri

Illustrations by BEATRICE DERWINSKI, BERYL JONES,
RUTH WOOD, *and* SISTER JOSEFA MARY, S.C.

Ginn and Company

BOSTON · NEW YORK · CHICAGO · ATLANTA · DALLAS · PALO ALTO · TORONTO

Reprinted by Seton Home Study School, 2011

Seton Home Study School
1350 Progress Drive
Front Royal, VA 22630
(540) 636-9990
(540) 636-1602 fax

Internet: www.setonhome.org
E-mail: info@setonhome.org

Front Cover: *Musical Angel with Viol*, Melozzo de Forli

DEDICATION

This book is dedicated
to St. Joseph the Workman,
Foster Father of the Son of God,
and Patron of the Universal Church

Acknowledgments

Acknowledgment is due to publishers, composers, and authors for permission to reprint songs and poems in this book, as follows:

The Commonweal, "The Juniper Tree" (words only) by Eileen Duggan; Cooperative Recreation Service, Inc., "All the Heavens Praise Thy Name," from *The Pagoda*; Crown Publishers, Inc., "The Troika," from *A Treasury of the World's Finest Folk Song*, collected and arranged by Leonhard Deutsch. Copyright 1942 by Leonhard Deutsch. Used by permission of Crown Publishers, Inc.; Gerald S. Doyle, Limited, "Let Me Fish off Cape St. Mary's" from *Old Time Songs of Newfoundland*; Dublin, Republic of Ireland, Department of Education, "Welcome the Savior" from *Dánta Dé*; Ginn and Company, "The Bluebird" (arrangement of music), "Christmas Bells" (music only), "Holiday Song," "Mother" (words), from the *Music Education Series*; Ginn and Company and the editors of *The World of Music*, "Give Us the Wintertime," "I Will Go with My Father a-Plowing," "A Jolly Sailor Boy," "Night in the Desert," "Rosy Boy, Posy Boy," "Slumber, Slumber," "Valley of Glencoe," "Village Chimes"; Ginn and Company and the editors of *Our Singing World*, "Bells above the Chapel," "Come, Lovely May," "Cotton Needs Picking," "A Greeting," "Indian Summer," "Little Mohee," "Oh My, Oh Me," "Red River Valley," "Stodola Pumpa" (words), "When Christ Was Born," "When Night Is Falling," "The Wind"; Ginn and Company, the poem "Snow in the City" by Rachel Lyman Field from *The Children's Bookshelf* compiled by B. R. Buckingham; The Liturgical Press, translation of "Te Lucis" and "Mary, We Greet Thee" from *Sunday Compline*; The Macmillan Company, "Bells Are Ringing" from the *Tone and Rhythm Series, Book 6*; Mrs. Flora McDowell, "Shuckin' of the Corn"; McLaughlin & Reilly Company, "O Mary of Graces" (words) from *The Pius X Hymnal*, used by permission of McLaughlin & Reilly Company, copyright owners; W. W. Norton & Company, Inc., "Come, All Ye Young Sailormen" and "South Australia Is My Home" reprinted from *Songs of American Sailormen* by Joanna C. Colcord, copyright 1938 by W. W. Norton & Company, Inc.; Polanie Club, "The Quail Song" from *Treasures of Polish Songs*; The Ronald Press, "In the Valley" from *The Ballad Tree*, copyright 1950 the Ronald Press Company; G. Schirmer, Inc., "Prayer of the Norwegian Child," by Olaf Trojorgson, used by permission of G. Schirmer, Inc.; Ruth Crawford Seeger, "Tennessee," transcribed from Library of Congress recording by Ruth C. Seeger; Most Reverend Ambrose Senyshyn, O.S.B.M., Apostolic Exarch of Stamford, Connecticut, for his translation of "The Doxology" and "Lord Have Mercy" from The Divine Liturgy of the Byzantine Slav Rite; Janet E. Tobitt, "The Gay Caballero" from *Sing Me Your Song O!* and "Zither and I" from *Yours for a Song*.

"The Merry Lark" is from *Sing Together*, published by the Girl Scouts of the U.S.A.

In the case of some poems for which acknowledgment is not given, we have earnestly endeavored to find the original source and to procure permission for their use, but without success.

The contents of this book have received the approval of the DIOCESAN MUSIC COMMISSION, Boston, Massachusetts.

Contents

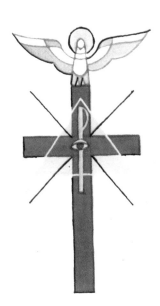

After Pentecost

God be in my head and in my understanding;
God be in mine eyes and in my looking;
God be in my mouth and in my speaking;
God be in my heart and in my thinking;
God be in my life and in my departing.

Sarum Primer, 1558

Hymn to the Holy Trinity

TRADITIONAL

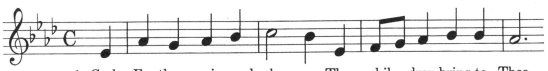

1. God, Fa - ther, praise and glo - ry Thy chil - dren bring to Thee.
2. And Thou, Lord Co - e - ter - nal, God's sole — be - got - ten Son.
3. O Ho - ly Ghost, Cre - a - tor, Thou gift — of God most high;

Good will and peace to man - kind shall now — for - ev - er be.
O Je - sus, King a - noint - ed Who has — re - demp - tion won.
Life, love and ho - ly wis - dom, our weak - ness now sup - ply.

1,2,3. O Most Ho - ly Trin - i - ty, Un - di - vid - ed — U - ni - ty,

Ho - ly God, Might - y God, God Im - mor - tal, be a - dored.

1

Cotton Needs Picking

Lively, two swings to a measure

VIRGINIA FOLK SONG

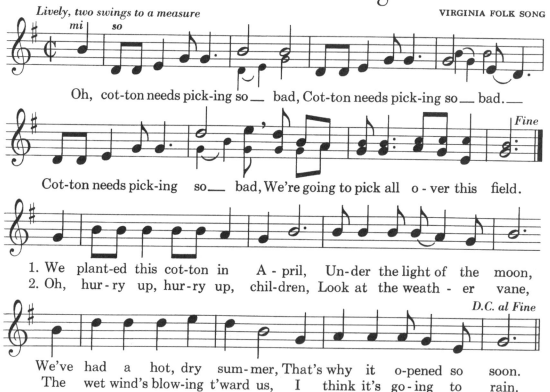

Oh, cot-ton needs pick-ing so __ bad, Cot-ton needs pick-ing so __ bad. __

Cot-ton needs pick-ing so __ bad, We're going to pick all o - ver this field.

Fine

1. We plant-ed this cot-ton in A - pril, Un-der the light of the moon,
2. Oh, hur-ry up, hur-ry up, chil-dren, Look at the weath - er vane,

D.C. al Fine

We've had a hot, dry sum-mer, That's why it o-pened so soon.
The wet wind's blow-ing t'ward us, I think it's go-ing to rain.

When there is one sharp in the key signature, *do* is on the second line.
D. C. al Fine means to repeat from the beginning and sing to *Fine*.

2

Shuckin' of the Corn

TENNESSEE FOLK SONG

With spirit

1. I have a ship on the o-cean ___ All lined with sil-ver and gold, ___
2. The wind blows cold in ___ Cai-ro, ___ The sun re-fus-es to shine. ___

do . . . do . . . do . . . . do . . . do . . . . . so . .

Be-fore I'd see my true love suf-fer That ship should be an-chored and sold. ___
Be-fore I'd see my true love suf-fer I'd work all the sum - mer time. ___

do . . do . . . fa . . . fa . . . . . do . . . . . . so . . . . . . do . .

Chorus

I'm a - go-in' to the shuck-in' of the corn, ___ I'm a - go-in' to the

do . . . . do . . . . . . do . . . . do . . . . . .

shuck-in' of the corn, ___ A - shuck-in' of the corn and a -

do . . . . .so . . . . . . .do . . . . . . do . . . . .

blow-in' of the horn, I'm a - go-in' to the shuck-in' of the corn. ___

fa . . . . .fa . . . . . .do . . . . . so . . . . . . do . . . . .

When there are sharps in the key signature, the last sharp to the right is *ti*.
Count up or down to find *do*. Where is high *do*? Where is low *do*?

The More We Get Together

Happily

The more we get to - geth - er, to - geth - er, to - geth - er;
do . . . . do . . . . so . . . . do . . . .

The more we get to - geth - er, the hap - pier are we!
do . . . . do . . . . so . . . . do

For your friends are my friends and my friends are your friends.
so . . . . do . . . . so . . . . do . . . .

The more we get to - geth - er, the hap - pier are we!
do . . . . do . . . . so . . . . do

This song is in the key of F Major. A major key takes its name from *do*. Here is the F Major scale:

do   re   mi   fa   so   la   ti   do
F   G   A   B♭   C   D   E   F

After you have sung the *chording tones* with syllables, sing the same tones with the words in the rhythm of the melody.

Old Irish Prayer

From the OLD IRISH
by THOMAS WALSH

MARYBETH BAYLEY

May the sweet name of Je-sus be lov-ing-ly grav-en On my heart's in-most ha-ven,

O__ Ma-ry, my Moth-er, Be Je-sus my Broth-er, And__ I, Je-sus' broth-er!

A bind-ing of love that no dis-tance can sev-er,

Be be-tween us for-ev-er, O my Sav-ior for-ev-er!

O Mary of Graces

GAELIC
Translated by DOUGLAS HYDE

IRISH FOLK SONG

1. O__ Ma-ry of __ grac-es and Moth-er of God, May I tread in the
2. And may-est thou save me by __ land and by sea, And may-est thou

paths that the right-eous have trod, And__ may-est thou save me from
save me from tor-tures to be. May the guard of the an-gels a-

E-vil's con-trol, And may-est thou save me in bod-y and soul.
bove me a-bide, May God be be-fore me and God at my side.

Sing this hymn with syllables.
Which syllable of the scale is omitted?

5

Salve Regina

do   mi   so

Sál - ve, Re - gí - na, Má - ter mi - se - ri - cór - di - ae: Ví - ta, dul - cé - do,

et spes nó - stra, sál - ve. Ad te cla - má - mus, éx - su - les,

fí - li - i Hé - vae. Ad te sus - pi - rá - mus, ge - mén - tes et flén - tes

in hac la - cri - má - rum vál - le. E - ia er - go, Ad - vo - cá - ta nó - stra,

íl - los tú - os mi - se - ri - cór - des ó - cu - los ad nos con - vér - te.

Et Jé - sum, be - ne - dí - ctum frú - ctum vén - tris tú - i, nó - bis post

hoc ex - sí - li - um o - stén - de. O clé - mens, O pí - a,

O dúl - cis Vír - go Ma - rí - a.

Can you find these neums in this hymn?
— podatus
— clivis
— torculus
— quilisma

6

Mary, We Greet Thee (Salve Regina)

do mi so

Ma - ry, we greet thee, Moth-er and Queen all mer-ci-ful, Our life, our sweet-ness

and our hope, we hail — thee. To thee we ex-iles, chil-dren of

Eve, lift our cry-ing. To thee we send our sighs as, mourn-ing and weep-ing,

we pass through this vale of sor-row. Haste, then, we pray. O our in-ter-ces-sor,

look with pit - y, with eyes of love com-pas-sion-ate, up-on us sin - ners.

And aft - er, when this earth-ly ex - ile shall be end-ed, show us thine

own most bless-ed Fruit, thy Je - sus, O — clem-ent, O — lov-ing,

The *so-fa* syllables are the same whether you sing from modern or chant notation.

O — most sweet Vir - gin Ma - ry.

7

Delight of the loving,
Dispeller of sadness,
Let the Church as a herald
Give honor to Mary.

Glorious Trinity,
Undivided Unity,
For the sake of Mary,
Save us forever.

Sometimes chant is conducted with movements of the hand. This is called *chironomy*. The upward movement, which helps give life or energy to chant, is called an *arsis* ⌒⌣. The downward movement, which gives a feeling of quiet or repose, is called a *thesis* ⌒⌣.

A chant is divided into rhythmic groups by counting 1–2, or 1–2–3. Each group should be conducted with either an *arsis* or a *thesis*. A slight "lift" made in a thesis, necessary because of the accented syllable of a word, is called an *undulation*.

Since, at this time, it is too difficult to learn all the rules for placing an *arsis* or a *thesis*, the chironomy will be marked for you. A rising melody is usually given an *arsis* and a descending melody, a *thesis*.

Concordi Laetitia

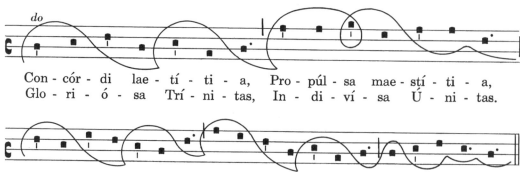

Con - cór - di lae - tí - ti - a, Pro - púl - sa mae - stí - ti - a,
Glo - ri - ó - sa Trí - ni - tas, In - di - ví - sa Ú - ni - tas.

Ma - rí - ae prae - có - ni - a Ré - co - lat Ec - clé - si - a: Vír - go Ma - rí - a.
Ob Ma - rí - ae mé - ri - ta, Nos sál - va per sáe - cu - la: Vír - go Ma - rí - a.

Try to do the chironomy while you sing this chant. There are two counts for every *arsis* or *thesis*. Notice the two *arses* in succession above "Propulsa"; notice also the *undulation* in "Virgo Maria."

8

Angeli Dei

An - ge - li Dé - i, qui cú - stos es mé - i, me tí - bi
(Angel of God, my guide, *to Whom*

com - mís - sum, pi - e - tá - te su - pér - na; il - lú - mi - na
I am committed by divine love,) *(enlighten me,*

cu - stó - di, ré - ge et gu - bér - na. A - men.
guard me, *and be with me.)*

This chant has no time signature: it is in free rhythm. Quarter notes are held
twice as long as eighth notes.

A Hymn of Praise

BLESSED PHILIP HOWARD   SISTER CECILIA, S.C.

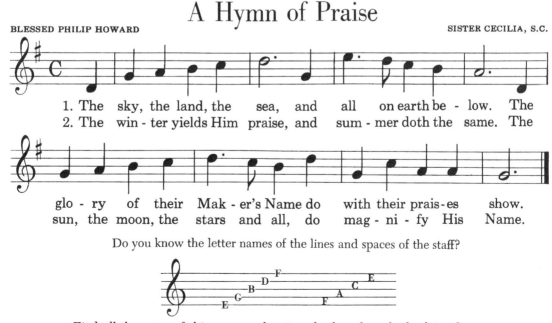

1. The sky, the land, the sea, and all on earth be - low. The
2. The win - ter yields Him praise, and sum - mer doth the same. The

glo - ry of their Mak - er's Name do with their prais - es show.
sun, the moon, the stars and all, do mag - ni - fy His Name.

Do you know the letter names of the lines and spaces of the staff?

Find all the notes of this song on the piano keyboard on the back inside cover
of your book.

9

Little Mohee

MOUNTAIN SONG

1. I once was a stran-ger, ___ and far from my home, ___ And
2. She sat down be-side me ___ and held out her hand ___ To
3. "Oh no, fair-est maid-en, ___ that nev-er could be. ___ My

in a strange coun-try, ___ 'way o-ver the foam. ___ As
give me a wel-come ___ to that beau-ti-ful land. ___ "My
ship soon is sail-ing ___ back o-ver the sea, ___ And

I sat a-wait-ing ___ the time for to pass, ___ I
fa-ther's a chief-tain, ___ my name is Mo-hee." ___ She
I have a sweet-heart ___ who's wait-ing for me, ___ Whose

saw com-ing near me ___ such a fair In-dian lass. ___
said, "Let us mar-ry; ___ make your home here with me." ___
heart is as faith-ful ___ as ___ an-y could be." ___

4. 'Twas early one morning, one morning in May,
   Her heart was most broken when these words I did say:
   "It's now I must leave you, so farewell, my dear,
   My ship sails are spreading and home I must steer."

5. The last time I saw her was down on the sand.
   My ship started homeward, she waved her hand.
   She called, "When you're home, dear, far over the blue,
   Remember I always will be waiting for you."

6. The girl I had trusted proved untrue to me.
   None here can compare with my little Mohee,
   So soon I'll be sailing far o'er the blue sea
   To live all my days with the little Mohee.

The key of C has no sharps or flats in the signature.
How many times does the tonic chord, C-E-G, occur?

Red River Valley

COWBOY SONG

The natural sign (♮) in the alto part, fifth line, changes F♯ to F.
The syllable name is changed from *ti* to *te*.

Panis Angelicus

ST. THOMAS AQUINAS

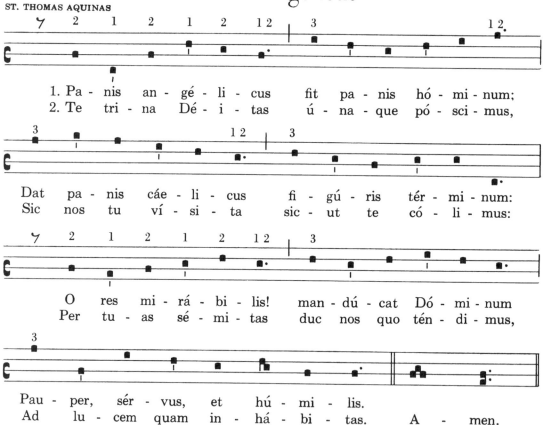

1. Pa - nis an - gé - li - cus fit pa - nis hó - mi - num;
2. Te tri - na Dé - i - tas ú - na - que pó - sci - mus,

Dat pa - nis cáe - li - cus fi - gú - ris tér - mi - num:
Sic nos tu ví - si - ta sic - ut te có - li - mus:

O res mi - rá - bi - lis! man - dú - cat Dó - mi - num
Per tu - as sé - mi - tas duc nos quo tén - di - mus,

Pau - per, sér - vus, et hú - mi - lis.
Ad lu - cem quam in - há - bi - tas. A - men.

The Bread of Angels becomes the bread of men.
The bread of Heaven fulfills the prophetic types.
O wondrous truth! The poor, the lowly,
And the slave upon their Master feed.

Thee, Godhead, One and Three, we pray,
Come Thou to visit us, as we our homage pay.
Be Thine the path, and Thou our guide, as we journey
To the light where Thou dost dwell.

Count the rhythm of this hymn. Begin with "rest two." The ictus mark is always "one." Sometimes the count is carried over a quarter or half bar for "three." On the next page you will find the same hymn in modern notation.

12

Panis Angelicus

ST. THOMAS AQUINAS

1. Pa - nis an - gé - li - cus fit pa - nis hó - mi - num;
2. Te tri - na Dé - i - tas ú - na - que pó - sci - mus,

Dat pa - nis cáe - li - cus fi - gú - ris tér - mi - num:
Sic nos tu ví - si - ta sic - ut te có - li - mus:

O res mi - rá - bi - lis! man - dú - cat Dó - mi - num
Per tu - as sé - mi - tas duc nos quo tén - di - mus,

Pau - per, sér - vus, et hú - mi - lis.
Ad lu - cem quam in há - bi - tas. A - men.

The counting in modern notation is the same as in chant notation.

13

Caisson Song

UNITED STATES ARMY SONG

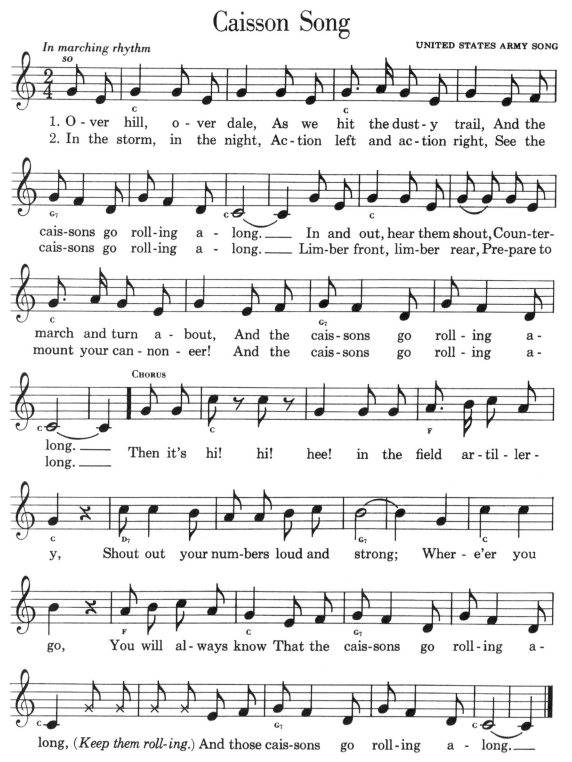

In marching rhythm

1. O - ver hill, o - ver dale, As we hit the dust - y trail, And the
2. In the storm, in the night, Ac - tion left and ac - tion right, See the

cais-sons go roll-ing a - long. —— In and out, hear them shout, Coun-ter-
cais-sons go roll-ing a - long. —— Lim-ber front, lim-ber rear, Pre-pare to

march and turn a - bout, And the cais - sons go roll - ing a -
mount your can - non - eer! And the cais - sons go roll - ing a -

CHORUS

long. —— Then it's hi! hi! hee! in the field ar - til - ler -
long. ——

y, Shout out your num-bers loud and strong; Wher - e'er you

go, You will al - ways know That the cais-sons go roll-ing a -

long, (*Keep them roll-ing.*) And those cais-sons go roll-ing a - long. ——

The Quail Song

JOSEPH CONTOSKI

POLISH FOLK TUNE

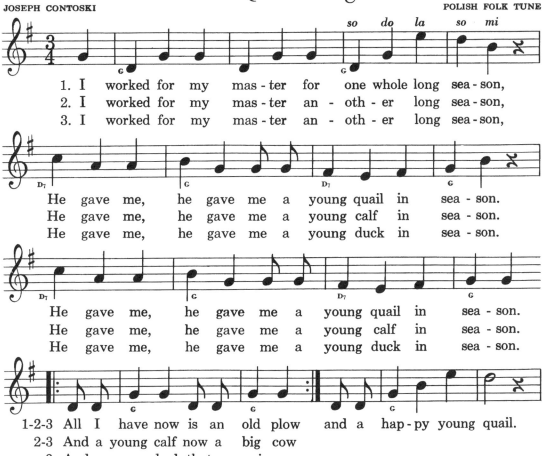

so do la so mi

1. I worked for my mas-ter for one whole long sea-son,
2. I worked for my mas-ter an-oth-er long sea-son,
3. I worked for my mas-ter an-oth-er long sea-son,

He gave me, he gave me a young quail in sea-son.
He gave me, he gave me a young calf in sea-son.
He gave me, he gave me a young duck in sea-son.

He gave me, he gave me a young quail in sea-son.
He gave me, he gave me a young calf in sea-son.
He gave me, he gave me a young duck in sea-son.

1-2-3 All I have now is an old plow and a hap-py young quail.
2-3 And a young calf now a big cow
3 And a young duck that can swim now

Fly-ing-o, fly-ing-o, all a-bout my land-o.

A light, fast song in $\frac{3}{4}$ time sounds best when sung with one swing to a measure.

Make New Friends

FOUR-PART ROUND

Make new friends, but keep the old.— One is sil-ver and the oth-er gold.

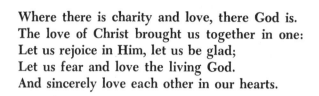

Where there is charity and love, there God is.
The love of Christ brought us together in one:
Let us rejoice in Him, let us be glad;
Let us fear and love the living God.
And sincerely love each other in our hearts.

Ubi Caritas

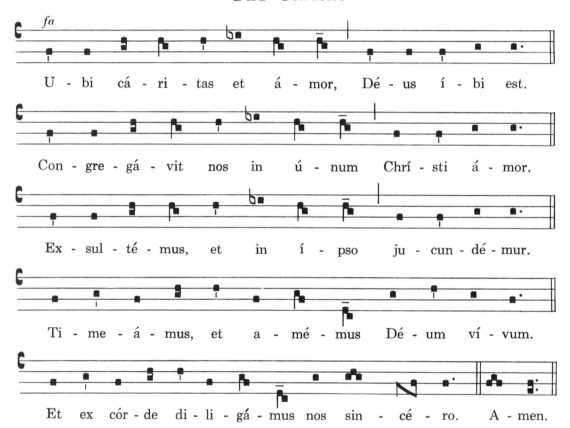

U - bi cá - ri - tas et á - mor, Dé - us í - bi est.

Con - gre - gá - vit nos in ú - num Chrí - sti á - mor.

Ex - sul - té - mus, et in í - pso ju - cun - dé - mur.

Ti - me - á - mus, et a - mé - mus Dé - um ví - vum.

Et ex cór - de di - li - gá - mus nos sin - cé - ro. A - men.

Count the rhythmic groups of two and three while you sing this chant. The
ictus tells you to begin with "one." You will notice that there is no ictus on
many of the neums, because the first note of a neum is usually the first note of a
rhythmic group.

Godhead here in hiding, Whom I do adore,
Masked by these bare shadows, shape and nothing more,
See, Lord, at Thy service low lies here a heart
Lost, all lost in wonder at the God Thou art.

Jesus, Whom I look at shrouded here below,
I beseech Thee send me what I thirst for so,
Some day to gaze on Thee face to face in light
And be blest forever with Thy glory's sight.

Translated by G. B. Hopkins

Adoro Te Devote

1. A - dó - ro te de - vó - te, la - tens Dé - i - tas, Quae sub his
fi - gú - ris vé - re lá - ti - tas: Tí - bi se cor mé - um
tó - tum súb - ji - cit, Qui - a, te con - tém-plans, tó - tum dé - fi - cit.

A - men.

2. Jésu, quem velátum nunc aspício,
Oro fiat illud quod tam sitio;
Ut te reveláta cérnens fácie,
Visu sim beátus túae glóriae.   Amen.

Try to do the chironomy while singing this chant. Notice the two arses in
succession in the first line above "Adoro te" as well as in the second line above
"Tibi se cor." Notice also that the arsis in the second line above "se cor" has
three counts. Be sure to give each note one count.

17

In the Harvest Time

SISTER CECILIA, S. C.

LEBANESE FOLK TUNE

la

1. Now the gold-en grain is___ gath-ered in And the grapes are ripe on the
2. To the Lord Who gives the har-vest time Be___ prais-es now and for-

hill-side, And the ol-ive trees in the val-ley stand With a
ev-er, To___ Him Who gave the___ sun___ and rain Your___

har-vest full and fine.
joy-ful voic-es___ raise.

CHORUS

In the har-vest time, in the har-vest time;

Time for joy and mer-ri-ment and song. In the har-vest time,

in the har-vest time, Neigh-bors come and join in mer-ry song.

This song is in a minor key. The first melody note is *la*. Since *la* is on G, the song is in the key of g minor.

Praise the Lord

TRADITIONAL HEBREW MELODY

1. Praise the Lord, the Lord to Whom all praise___ is due.
2. Bless the Lord, oh, bless His Name, His Ho - ly Name.

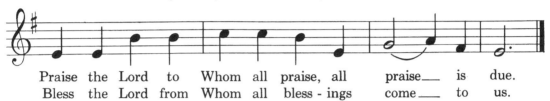

Praise the Lord to Whom all praise, all praise___ is due.
Bless the Lord from Whom all bless - ings come___ to us.

Do you hear that this song is in a minor key?
What is the syllable name of the last note?

King of Kings

ERICK VAN

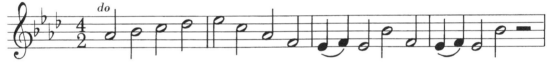

1. King of Kings, yet born of Ma-ry, As___ of old on earth He stood;
2. Rank on rank the host of heav-en Spreads its van-guard on the way,

Lord of Lords in hu-man ves-ture In___ the Bod-y and the Blood.
As the Light of Light de-scend-eth From the realms of end - less day,

He will give___ to all the faith - ful His own self for heav'n-ly food.
That the pow'rs of hell may van - ish As the dark-ness clears a - way.

The time signature tells you that there are 4 beats in a measure and a half note receives one beat. This is an unusual time signature.

How many quarter notes are sung to a beat?

Advent

 **ING** of Gentiles, their desire and the cornerstone that makest both one: COME·AND·REDEEM·MAN··· WHOM·THOU didst form out of the dust of the earth ✠ ✠ ✠

EPHESIANS 2,14,20.

Rorate Caeli

Ro - rá - te cáe - li dé - su - per, et nú - bes plú - ant jú - stum.
(*Drop down dew, ye heavens,* *and let the clouds rain the Just One.*)

O Come, O Come, Emmanuel

TRADITIONAL

1. O come, O come, Em - man - u - el, And ran - som cap - tive Is - ra - el,
2. O come, Thou Key of Da - vid, come And o - pen wide our heav'n - ly home,

That mourns in lone - ly ex - ile here Un - til the Son of God ap - pear.
Make safe the way to Heav - en's height, And close the way to end - less night.

Re - joice! __ Re - joice! __ O Is - ra - el, To thee shall come Em - man - u - el.

The Lord Is My Shepherd

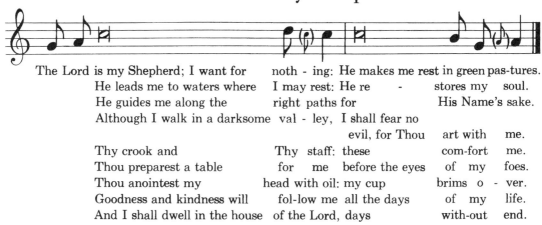

The Lord is my Shepherd; I want for noth - ing: He makes me rest in green pas-tures.
He leads me to waters where I may rest: He re - stores my soul.
He guides me along the right paths for His Name's sake.
Although I walk in a darksome val - ley, I shall fear no
evil, for Thou art with me.
Thy crook and Thy staff: these com-fort me.
Thou preparest a table for me before the eyes of my foes.
Thou anointest my head with oil: my cup brims o - ver.
Goodness and kindness will fol-low me all the days of my life.
And I shall dwell in the house of the Lord, days with-out end.

Creator Alme Siderum

1. Cre - á - tor ál - me sí - de-rum, Ae - tér - na lux cre-dén - ti - um,
2. Vír - tus, hó - nor, laus, gló - ri - a Dé - o Pá - tri cum Fí - li - o,

Jé - su, Re-dém-ptor ó - mni-um, In - tén-de vó - tis súp-pli-cum.
Sán - cto sí - mul Pa - rá - cli - to, In sae-cu - ló-rum saé - cu - la. A - men.

Bountiful Creator of the skies,
Eternal light of those who believe in Thee,
Jesus, Redeemer of all,
Heed the prayers of Thy suppliants.

Power, honor, praise, and glory
To God the Father with the Son,
And likewise to the Holy Paraclete,
World without end.

Try to do the chironomy while you sing this hymn.
Notice the two arses in succession in the first and last phrase.
Fa is on the third line.

21

Hear, O Father

TRADITIONAL HEBREW

Hear, O Fa-ther, hear our pray'r, From our hearts it soars to

Thee; Teach us, God, our du-ties all, Thee to seek, Thy love to

see; True to be, and good and kind, Pure in heart and soul and mind.

Be careful to sing the dotted-quarter-and-eighth-note rhythm pattern correctly.

All the Birds Have Flown Away

SISTER CECILIA, S. C.

FINNISH FOLK TUNE

1. All the birds have flown a-way, All the leaves have fall-en.
2. Lakes are fro-zen, woods are still; Fields are white and si-lent.

Now the north wind brings the snow, Brings the frost-y win-ter.
Heav-y, heav-y falls the snow In the frost-y win-ter.

In some measures of this song, *so*, the seventh tone of the minor scale is raised by a sharp (♯), and becomes *si*. Notes thus preceded by a sharp (♯), a natural (♮), or a flat (♭), are called *chromatics*. Sing the song with syllables.

From Whose Abundant Stores

From the oratorio "THE SEASONS"
FRANZ JOSEPH HAYDN

Rather slowly

From Whose a-bun-dant stores, the earth with plen-ty flows,

And Whose al-might-y love ____ makes glad the heart of man.

Our end - less praise we give Thee, Al - might - y Lord of all. __

Our end - less praise we sing to Thee, Al - might - y Lord of all.

How Many Camels Did You See?

PALESTINIAN ROUND

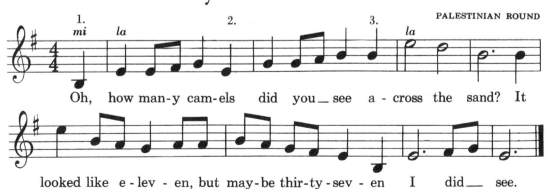

Oh, how man-y cam-els did you __ see a - cross the sand? It

looked like e - lev - en, but may-be thir-ty-sev - en I did __ see.

Is this round in a major or a minor key?

23

Legend of Christ as a Beggar

la ti do re mi

FRENCH FOLK SONG

1. At the door a poor man is stand-ing,
2. Of-ten in the clothes of a poor man
Je-sus Christ s'ha-bille en ____ pau-vre:

Ask-ing of your char - i - ty.
Christ will ask your char - i - ty.
Fai - tes-moi la cha - ri - té!

Dressed in shab-by clothes he is plead-ing:
He will come to beg at your win-dow:
Je - sus Christ s'ha-bille en ____ pau-vre:

Cold and hun-gry too is ____ he.
Cold and hun-gry He will ____ be.
Fai - tes - moi la cha - ri - té!

la

O - pen wide your heart and o-pen wide the door,
O - pen wide your heart and bid Him en - ter there.
Des miet-tes de vo - tre ta - - - ble.

Give him food and drink from your store.
Of - fer Him your love and your care.
Je fe - rai bien mon dî - ner.

24

Hail, O Star of Ocean

OLD HYMN

S. R. M.

1. Hail, O star of o - cean, O Ma - ri - a!
2. With thy Son, our Sav - ior, O Ma - ri - a!
3. Praise to God the Fa - ther, O Ma - ri - a!

Maid - en pure and low - ly, O Ma - ri - a!
Be our in - ter - ces - sor, O Ma - ri - a!
To our Sav - ior, hon - or, O Ma - ri - a!

Ev - er sin - less vir - gin, O Ma - ri - a!
Beg for us His mer - cy, O Ma - ri - a!
To the Ho - ly Spir - it, O Ma - ri - a!

Gate of heav - en ho - ly, O Ma - ri - a!
Beg for us for - give - ness, O Ma - ri - a!
Bless - ings be and glo - ry, O Ma - ri - a!

All the Heavens Praise Thy Name

CHINESE HYMN

1. All the heav-ens praise Thy name, All the earth Thy peace has won,
2. All true good-ness comes from Thee, All true wis-dom sings of Thee,

All men glo - ri - fy Thee, Lord, God Tri-une, the E - ter - nal One.
All true rev-'rence ends in Thee, Ho - ly Light the Al-might-y One.

The Chinese often use a five-tone scale: *do re mi so la.* This is called a *pentatonic scale.*

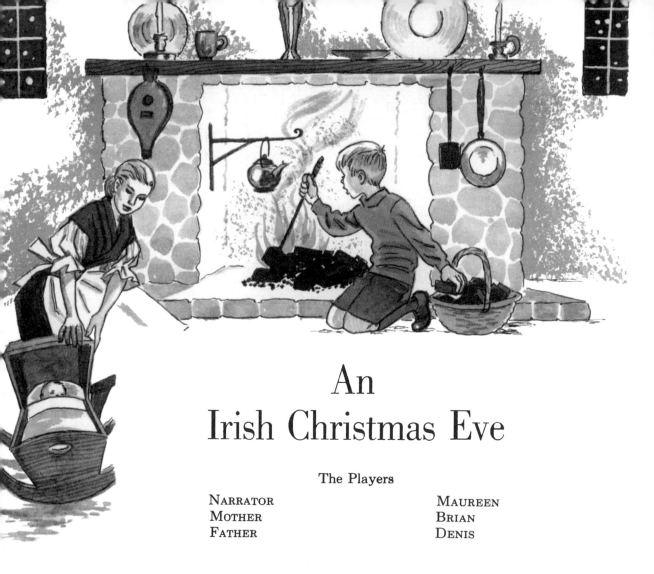

An
Irish Christmas Eve

The Players

NARRATOR	MAUREEN
MOTHER	BRIAN
FATHER	DENIS

NARRATOR. In the country villages of Ireland, Christmas Eve is a day of great preparation for the coming of the Savior. All the houses have been cleaned and whitewashed inside and out, until they shine as white as snow against the green hillsides. The mother of the family has been busy making pats of fresh butter for the poor people of the village, and baking many loaves of good raisin bread for the big breakfast after the Midnight Mass. Let us go into an Irish kitchen on Christmas Eve and see what is happening there.

(*We see a great stone fireplace, where a peat fire is burning brightly. A boy kneels beside it, stirring up the coals and adding bricks of peat from a basket beside him. There are a table and a few chairs. The mother is sitting on a low stool near the fireplace, rocking a cradle as she sings a lullaby.*)

Lullaby

ALFRED GRAVES

IRISH FOLK TUNE

1. I've found my bon-ny babe a nest on Slum-ber Tree. I'll
2. I'd put my pret-ty child to float a-way from me, With-

rock you there to ros-y rest, a - store ma - chree! Hush-
in the sil-ver new moon's boat on Slum-ber Sea! Hush-

1,2. Hush-o, hush-o,

o, hush-o, Oh, lull-a-lo sing all the
o, hush-o, And when your star-ry sail is

hush-o, Hush-o, hush-o,

leaves On Slum-ber Tree, on Slum-ber Tree Till ev-'ry
o'er From Slum-ber Sea, from Slum-ber Sea, My pre-cious

Hush-o, hush-o,

thing that hurts or grieves A-far must flee, a-far must
one you'll step to shore On Moth-er's knee, on Moth-er's

Hush-o, Hush-o, hush-o.

flee. Hush - o, hush - o.
knee. Hush - o, hush - o.

27

MOTHER.   Brian, go and see what is keeping Maureen. She is a
long time bringing the butter pats from the dairy.

MAUREEN.   (*At the door*) Here I am, Mother, and here is the butter.
(*She lays the butter pats on the table.*) Here is one for old
Mrs. McGuire, and one for the Sullivan family, and one
for blind Patrick, and one for - - - who else, Mother?
There is an extra one.

MOTHER.   That one is for the new neighbors. They haven't a cow,
so we must give them Christmas butter.

MAUREEN.   Oh, yes, young Tom and Molly Shanahan, who live in
the last house down the road. Christmas butter for the
Shanahans this year. (*She is wrapping the butter pats in
clean towels as she talks.*) Now, where can Denis be?
He promised me he'd bring the holly branches when he
came home from confession. Great sins, indeed, he
must have, to be talking so long! (*Outside a boy's voice
is heard singing, "Come Buy My Nice Fresh Holly."*)

Come, Buy My Nice Fresh Holly

IRISH FOLK TUNE

1. Come, buy my nice fresh hol-ly, and my hol-ly sprigs so
2. Oh, won't you buy my hol-ly, 'tis the love-li-est e'er

green. I have the fin-est branch-es that ev-er yet were
seen? And won't you buy my i-vy so shin-ing and

seen. Come, buy from me, good Chris-tians, come, buy from me, I
green? Oh, buy just a lit-tle branch of each, just a ti-ny sprig, I

pray. And I'll wish you a Mer-ry Christ-mas and a Hap-py New Year's Day.
pray. And may God send a bless-ed Christ-mas and a Hap-py New Year's Day.

BRIAN. Here comes Denis now.

(DENIS *comes in, his arms filled with holly branches. He keeps singing the song, in which all join him, and pretends to sell the holly.*)

MAUREEN. Stop fooling now, Denis, and help me put up the holly.
(MAUREEN *and the boys decorate the fireplace. As they work they sing, "Oh, Hang Up the Holly.")*

Oh, Hang Up the Holly

IRISH CAROL

1. Oh, hang up the hol - ly so fresh and so green,
2. Oh, deep is the si - lence on moun - tains so green,

For a bless - ed Mer - ry Christ-mas and Hap - py New Year.
May the dear Lord send you bless - ings through-out the New Year.

Put a can - dle so bright in the win - dow to - night,
Should ___ Ma - ry and Jo - seph be trav'l - ing this night

For a bless - ed Mer - ry Christ-mas and Hap - py New Year.
They will bless you for the can - dle - light burn - ing so clear.

May the bless - ing of God be up - on you this night,
It will lead them to shel - ter and wel - come so bright,

And I wish you Mer - ry Christ-mas and Hap - py New Year.
And I wish you Mer - ry Christ-mas and Hap - py New Year.

MOTHER.	Your father is late with the milking. Go help him, Brian; it is supper time. (*She begins to set the table.*)
BRIAN.	Here comes Father now. I'll help him with the milk pail.
FATHER.	(*Entering*) Well, Mother, I have a surprise for you. Your little brown cow has given you a Christmas gift, twin heifers.
MOTHER.	Blessed be God!
MAUREEN.	Oh, two little calves on Christmas Eve! What shall we name them?
FATHER.	Pegeen is your mother's cow, so Mother must name the twins.
MOTHER.	It is something I must think about, and you must all stop shouting or you'll waken the baby. (*She goes on setting the table, while Father takes off his coat and pours milk from the pail into a big pitcher.*)
FATHER.	The calves are brown, like Pegeen, but one has a white star on its forehead.
MOTHER.	When they are weaned we must give one of them to the Shanahans. That way we can thank God for His goodness.
FATHER.	Indeed He has been good to us.

MOTHER. Now, Maureen, open the door; it is growing dark. (*They all stand around the table while* MAUREEN *opens the door.*)

FATHER. Fasten the door tightly, Maureen, so that it will not blow shut. On this night the Holy Virgin and good Saint Joseph walked the road to Bethlehem and found the doors closed against them. Never must the door of an Irish house be closed on Christmas Eve. Brian, bring the Christmas candle. (BRIAN *brings a tall candle and sets it on the table. The father takes a taper and lights it at the fire, then lights the candle.* [*Electric candles may be substituted.*]])

FATHER. God be praised for light!

ALL. May He give us the light of Heaven!

FATHER. Set the candle in the window, Denis, so that the Mother of God will know she is welcome in this house. (DENIS *carries the candle to the window, while all sing,* "Welcome the Savior.")

Welcome the Savior

Translated by JAMES MARTIN

OLD IRISH CAROL

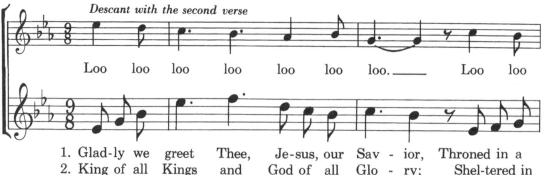

Descant with the second verse

Loo   loo   loo   loo   loo   loo   loo.___   Loo   loo

1. Glad-ly we   greet   Thee,   Je-sus, our   Sav - ior,   Throned in a
2. King of all   Kings   and   God of all   Glo - ry;   Shel-tered in

loo loo loo loo loo. ___ Loo loo loo loo loo

man - ger and cra - dled so low - ly Great Son of the Fa - ther in
sta - ble the shep-herds have found Thee, With them we a-dore Thee and

loo loo loo loo, Loo loo loo loo loo. ___

splen-dor e - ter - nal, Born of a maid - en, ___ Ma-ry, most ho - ly.
wel-come Thy com - ing, Child with the ra- diance of heav-en a-round Thee.

MOTHER.	And now we shall eat our supper, for the children must sleep a while before we go to the Midnight Mass.
MAUREEN.	There is raisin bread and fresh milk, and baked potatoes and our own good butter—
FATHER.	And fresh mackerel caught this morning, and a cup of tea—
DENIS.	And a goose roasting for our Christmas dinner to-morrow!
MOTHER.	God is good; let us never forget His goodness. (*They stand at their places, heads bowed, hands folded.*)
FATHER.	In the Name of the Father and of the Son and of the Holy Ghost.
ALL.	Amen.
FATHER.	Bless us, O Lord, and these Thy gifts which we have received from Thy bounty, through Christ, Our Lord.
ALL.	Amen.

(*They sit down at the table.*)

(*The chorus may repeat "Welcome the Savior."*)

THE END

Christmastide and After

While all things were in quiet silence, and the night was in the midst of her course, Thy almighty word leapt down from heaven from Thy royal throne.

Book of Wisdom

Angels We Have Heard on High

FRENCH CAROL

1. An-gels we have heard on high, Sweet-ly sing-ing o'er the plains;
2. Shep-herds, why this ju-bi-lee? Why your joy-ous songs pro-long?
3. Come to Beth-le-hem and see Him whose birth the an-gels sing;

And the moun-tains in re-ply Ech-o-ing their joy-ous strains.
What the glad-some ti-dings be Which in-spire your heav'n-ly song?
Come a-dore on bend-ed knee Christ the Lord, our new-born King.

CHORUS

Glo - ri-a in ex-cel-sis De-o,

Glo - ri-a in ex-cel-sis De-o.

Ecce Nomen Domini

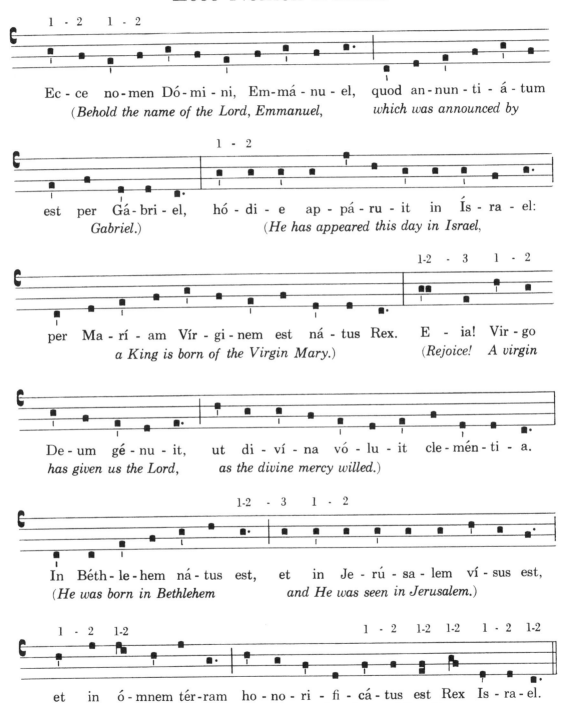

Ec - ce no-men Dó - mi - ni, Em-má - nu - el, quod an-nun - ti - á - tum
(Behold the name of the Lord, Emmanuel, which was announced by

est per Gá - bri - el, hó - di - e ap - pá - ru - it in Ís - ra - el:
Gabriel.) (He has appeared this day in Israel,

per Ma - rí - am Vír - gi - nem est ná - tus Rex. E - ia! Vir - go
a King is born of the Virgin Mary.) (Rejoice! A virgin

De - um gé - nu - it, ut di - ví - na vó - lu - it cle - mén - ti - a.
has given us the Lord, as the divine mercy willed.)

In Béth - le - hem ná - tus est, et in Je - rú - sa - lem ví - sus est,
(He was born in Bethlehem and He was seen in Jerusalem.)

et in ó - mnem tér - ram ho - no - ri - fi - cá - tus est Rex Is - ra - el.
(He was honored by the whole world as King of Israel.)

In the Valley

WHITE SPIRITUAL

Reverently

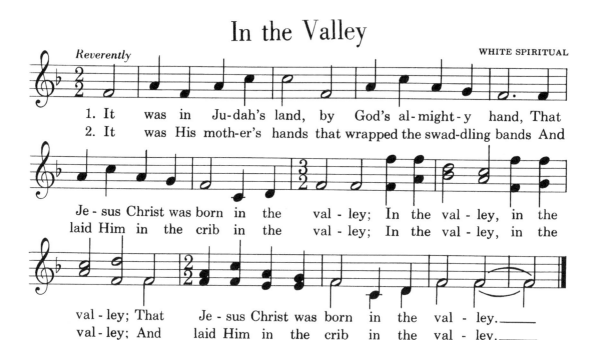

1. It was in Ju-dah's land, by God's al-might-y hand, That
2. It was His moth-er's hands that wrapped the swad-dling bands And

Je - sus Christ was born in the val - ley; In the val - ley, in the
laid Him in the crib in the val - ley; In the val - ley, in the

val - ley; That Je - sus Christ was born in the val - ley.____
val - ley; And laid Him in the crib in the val - ley.____

Notice the changes of time signature.

On the Road to Bethlehem

ROBERT HUGH BENSON

TRADITIONAL

1. Cold - ly blew the wind and snow On the road to Beth - le - hem.
2. Ere the night had passed to morn, In the town of Beth - le - hem.
3. East-ern kings are on their way To the town of Beth - le - hem.

Two there were that trav-eled slow, All that day_ so long a - go.
Rose the sun on us for-lorn; In the man - ger old and worn,
Shep-herds run ere break of day, At His feet their vows to pay,

On the road to Beth - le - hem.
In the town of Beth - le - hem.
In the town of Beth - le - hem.

Measures 6, 7, 14, and 15
have a natural sign, which
raises *fa* to *fi*.

Silent Night

Translated from the original by
FATHER JOSEPH MOHR

FRANZ GRUBER
ARRANGED

DESCANT

Oo (or hum)

1. Si - lent night, Ho - ly night, All is calm, all is bright,
2. Si - lent night, Ho - ly night, Shep-herds first see the light,

Oo

Round yon Vir - gin Moth-er and Child, Ho - ly In-fant so ten-der and mild.
Hear the Al - le - lu - ias ring, Which the an - gel cho - rus sing.

Oo   Oo

Sleep in heav-en-ly peace, —   Sleep in heav-en-ly peace. —
Christ, the Sav-ior, has come, —   Christ, the Sav-ior, has come. —

The Little Child Jesus,
He blesseth each thing;
The bud and the blossom,
The bird on the wing.
The sheep in the pasture,
The ox in the stall,
The Little Child Jesus
He loveth them all.

Our Lord Was Born in Bethlehem

Translated by H. M. H.

NORWEGIAN FOLK SONG

1. Our Lord was born in Beth-le-hem, a bless-ed, beau-ti-ful Boy,
2. The Ho-ly Child of Beth-le-hem was King of realms a-bove

His star was bright as a gold-en sun, His an-gels sang with joy.——
He came to lie in a man-ger bed and bring us peace and love.——

From Heaven High

TRANSLATED

GERMAN CRADLE SONG

1. From heav-en high the an-gels come, E - ia, E -
2. The an-gels sing a car-ol sweet, E - ia, E -

1. From heav-en high the an-gels
2. The an-gels sing a car-ol

ia! Su - sa - ni, su - sa - ni, su - sa - ni! They sing with
ia! Su - sa - ni, su - sa - ni, su - sa - ni! Be - hold the

come, Su - sa - ni, su - sa - ni, su - sa - ni! They
sweet, Su - sa - ni, su - sa - ni, su - sa - ni! Be -

joy to all ___ the earth, al - le - lu - ia, ___
Vir - gin Moth - er mild, al - le - lu - ia, ___

sing with joy ___ to all the earth, ___ al - le - lu
hold the Vir - gin Moth - er mild, ___ al - le - lu

___ Of our ___ Re - deem - er's ho - ly birth.
___ She rocks ___ to sleep ___ her Ho - ly Child.

ia, Of our ___ Re - deem - er's ho - ly birth.
ia, She rocks ___ to sleep her Ho - ly Child.

Sing this carol with one slow swing to a measure.
The key is G Major.
The tonic chord is G-B-D. Find it on your keyboard.

THE HURON CAROL

St. Jean de Brébeuf sat in his poor little hut trying to think of the best way to write a Christmas carol for his beloved Indians, the Hurons. He realized that he must refer to objects and use words familiar to the Indians. He knew that they would know what a "bark hut" was, but not a "stable"; what a piece of "rabbit fur" was, but not "swaddling clothes." They would understand better if the shepherds were "hunters" and the Three Kings, "Chiefs," whose gifts were "fox and beaver pelts" instead of gold, frankincense, and myrrh.

He wrote this beautiful carol in the Indians' own language and in a way that they could understand. The Indians could now sing about the birth of the Christ Child and could learn through song to know and love the Son of God.

St. Jean de Brébeuf, who was tortured to death by the Iroquois in 1649, is one of the great North American martyrs.

The Huron Carol

SAINT JEAN DE BRÉBEUF
Translation by J. E. MIDDLETON

HURON INDIAN CHRISTMAS CAROL

1. 'Twas in the moon of win - ter - time When all the birds had fled,
2. With - in a lodge of bro - ken bark The ten - der Babe was found,
3. O chil - dren of the for - est free, O sons of Man - i - tou,

That might-y Git-chi Man-i-tou Sent an-gel choirs in-stead;
A rag-ged robe of rab-bit skin En-wrapped His beau-ty 'round;
The Ho-ly Child of earth and Heav'n Is born to-day for you.

Be - fore their light the stars grew dim, And won-d'ring hunt-ers heard the hymn;
But as the hunt-er braves drew nigh, The an-gel song rang loud and high. —
Come kneel be-fore the ra-diant Boy Who brings you beau-ty, peace and joy. —

CHORUS

"Je-sus your King is born, Je-sus is born, Je-sus A - ha - ton - hi - a."

Joseph, Dearest Joseph Mine

From a GERMAN CHRISTMAS CAROL

SISTER JOHN JOSEPH, C.S.J.

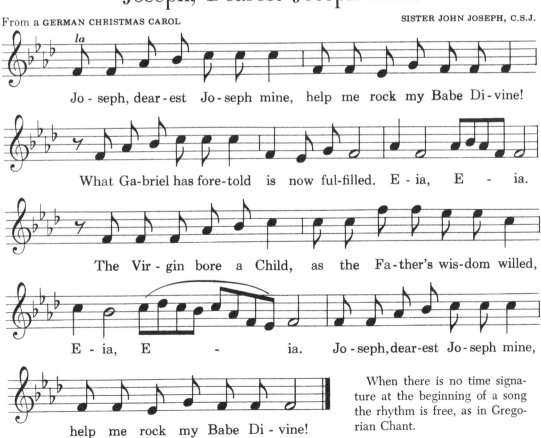

Jo - seph, dear - est Jo - seph mine, help me rock my Babe Di - vine!

What Ga - briel has fore - told is now ful - filled. E - ia, E - ia.

The Vir - gin bore a Child, as the Fa - ther's wis - dom willed,

E - ia, E - ia. Jo - seph, dear - est Jo - seph mine,

help me rock my Babe Di - vine!

When there is no time signature at the beginning of a song the rhythm is free, as in Gregorian Chant.

When Christ Was Born

English version by ROSS FABER

Rather slowly

NEAPOLITAN CAROL

1. When Christ, the Ho - ly Child was born in Beth - le - hem The
2. Up - on the earth was peace; up - on the earth was love; The
3. The shep - herd saw the light and lift - ed up ___ his head; An

night grew clear as noon-day, with ev - 'ry star a gem. Such a
sav - age moun-tain li - on ___ grew gen - tle as a dove, Wolves and
an - gel bright as morn-ing ap - peared to him and said, "Hear ye,

ra - diance, such a glo - ry, such a light was nev - er seen! And
calves and lambs and leop - ards all ___ in friend-ship went their way, And
shep - herd, hear ye, shep - herd, now re - joice and have no fear For

from the O - ri - ent ___ Came Wise Men trav-'ling hith - er ___ be -
on the peace - ful fields The bears and goats to - geth - er ___ were
Heav'n is come to earth. Be joy - ful, oh, be joy - ful ___ for

neath the star - ry sheen.
hap - pi - ly at play.
Christ our Lord is here."

When Handel was a young man he spent a few years in Italy. There he heard this carol sung by shepherds near Naples. Many years later in England he wrote "The Messiah." The memory of this Neapolitan carol undoubtedly influenced Handel when he composed the aria "He Shall Feed His Flock."

Christmas Bells

HENRY W. LONGFELLOW

WILL EARHART

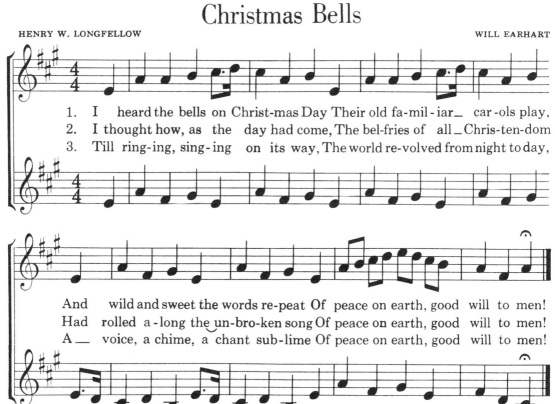

1. I heard the bells on Christ-mas Day Their old fa-mil-iar— car-ols play,
2. I thought how, as the day had come, The bel-fries of all—Chris-ten-dom
3. Till ring-ing, sing-ing on its way, The world re-volved from night to day,

And wild and sweet the words re-peat Of peace on earth, good will to men!
Had rolled a-long the un-bro-ken song Of peace on earth, good will to men!
A— voice, a chime, a chant sub-lime Of peace on earth, good will to men!

The alto has a bell-like melody pattern.
Can you find the place where the sopranos sing this pattern?

The Three Great Kings

PROVENÇAL FOLK TUNE

1,2. From a - far and fol-low-ing a star, The three great kings and all their train were

march - ing, From a - far and fol-low-ing a star, The three great

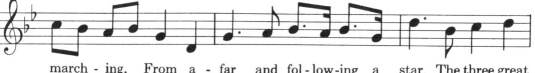

kings were march-ing on their way. Be-fore their eyes in the west-ern
Their treas-ures rare for a Child so

skies, The star shone bright, mov-ing stead-i-ly be - fore them. They sought a
fair They proud-ly bore o - ver des - ert and moun-tain. They sought a

Child Who was born a King, The three great kings who came from far a - way.
Child Who was born a King, The three great kings who came from far a - way.

As with Gladness Men of Old

W. C. DIX

CONRAD KOCHER

1. As with glad-ness men of old   Did the guid-ing star be-hold,
2. As with joy - ful steps they sped   To that low - ly man-ger bed,
3. As they of - fered gifts most rare   At that man-ger, rude and bare,

As with joy they hailed its light, Lead-ing on-ward, beam-ing bright,
There to __ bend the knee be-fore Him, Whom heav'n and earth a-dore,
So may we with hum - ble heart, And the joy that You im - part,

So, most gra-cious Lord, may we   Ev - er - more be led to Thee.
So may we with will - ing feet   Ev - er seek Thy mer - cy seat.
All our cost - ly treas-ures bring, Christ, to Thee, our Heav'n-ly King.

Find *do* from the key signature.
What is the letter name of the key?

Tu Es Petrus

Tu es Pé-trus, et su-per hanc pé-tram
(Thou art Peter,   and upon this rock

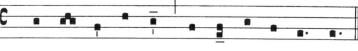

ae - di - fi - cá - bo   Ec - clé - si - am mé - am.
I will build   my church.)

How many neums in this chant do you recognize?

Kyrie

MASS XV

Ký - ri - e   e - lé - i - son. Ký - ri - e   e - lé - i - son. Ký - ri - e

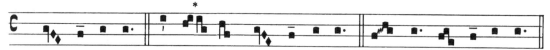

e - lé - i - son. Chrí - ste   e - lé - i - son. Chrí - ste e - lé - i - son.

Chrí - ste   e - lé - i - son. Ký - ri - e   e - lé - i - son.

Ký - ri - e   e - lé - i - son. Ký - ri - e   e - lé - i - son.

When a note and a neum, or two neums, come together on the same pitch and
the same vowel a *pressus* is formed. The *first* note of a *pressus* has the ictus. In
this chant each *pressus* is marked with an asterisk.

LUDWIG VAN BEETHOVEN

Ludwig van Beethoven was born in Bonn, Germany, on December 16, 1770. He was baptized in the parish church there on the following day. His mother, a lover of the beauty of nature, treated her children with understanding and kindness. His father, however, brought only unhappiness and poverty to the home, for he was a shiftless drunkard. His grandfather, a Flemish musician after whom Ludwig was named, was a court singer in Bonn. From this great man and fine musician Beethoven inherited his character and musical genius.

At the age of four, Ludwig started to study the clavier, an early type of piano. A little later he was also given lessons on the violin, then on the viola and organ. By the time he was eight years old, Beethoven played well enough to give public recitals in the concert halls of Cologne, Germany. Before he was eleven years old, Beethoven started to compose music; when he was only thirteen, he played for the rehearsals of court operas and was an assistant organist.

Beethoven was kindhearted, sympathetic, steadfast, and heroic; but he was also quick-tempered, over-sensitive, and sometimes abrupt. In spite of his faults, his friends remained loyal to him because they admired his good qualities and recognized his great genius. He knew Haydn and Mozart, both famous composers of the eighteenth century.

Before Beethoven was thirty years old, he realized that he was growing deaf. After some years he became totally deaf. His genius, however, was so great that in his mind he could "hear" the beautiful, majestic music he was composing. In this tragic deafness he wrote some of his greatest compositions. It is related that at a concert in which Beethoven conducted one of his symphonies, the audience was so impressed with the work that it became wild in its applause. Standing with his back to the audience, Beethoven could neither see nor hear the enthusiasm of the people. One of the players in the orchestra stood up and turned the great master around so that he could see the audience's response.

A week before his death Beethoven asked for a priest so that he could receive the Last Sacraments. He died on March 26, 1827.

Beethoven read and thought much; he loved poetry and the miracles God works in nature. He was a real student who was satisfied with nothing less than perfection in his works. He was one of the greatest composers of all times.

Mother

M. LOUISE BAUM

LUDWIG VAN BEETHOVEN

1. My moth-er's love is al-ways mine; So faith-ful to her child is she
2. If life should lead my feet a-stray, A-far and friend-less should I rove,

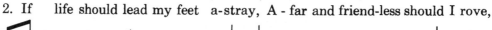

That hour by hour her heart re-turns To ten-der thoughts of — me. —
One love would still be true to me, My moth-er's change-less — love. —

What is the key of this song? What is the relative minor key?

A Garden in Winter

SISTER CECILIA, S.C.

LUDWIG VAN BEETHOVEN

Quietly and evenly

1. My gar-den in the sum-mer was a love-ly place to see,
2. But spring will come with wrens and rob-ins nest-ing in the eaves,

With mar-i-golds and la-dy-slip-pers bloom-ing there for me,
And all the trees will dress them-selves in new and shin-ing leaves,

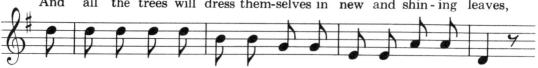

But now the sky is dark and gray and winds of win-ter blow,
For year by year, as win-ter goes, the spring comes back and then

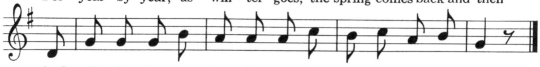

And all the flow-ers sleep be-neath the white and drift-ed snow.
In ev-'ry gar-den, ev-'ry heart, the flow-ers bloom a-gain.

Beethoven used the notes of the tonic chord of the key of G in the first two measures of this song. As you sing the song with syllables, notice how often you hear *do*, *mi*, and *so*. Find the tonic chord on the keyboard.

48

My Flesh is meat indeed, and My Blood is drink indeed:
He that eateth My Flesh and drinketh My Blood, abideth in Me, and I in him.

Tantum Ergo

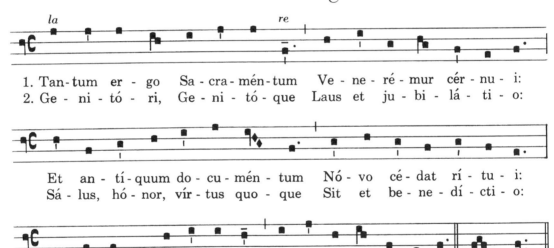

1. Tan-tum er-go Sa-cra-mén-tum Ve-ne-ré-mur cér-nu-i:
2. Ge-ni-tó-ri, Ge-ni-tó-que Laus et ju-bi-lá-ti-o:

Et an-tí-quum do-cu-mén-tum Nó-vo cé-dat rí-tu-i:
Sá-lus, hó-nor, vír-tus quo-que Sit et be-ne-dí-cti-o:

Prae-stet fí-des sup-ple-mén-tum Sén-su-um de-fé-ctu-i.
Pro-ce-dén-ti ab u-tró-que Cóm-par sit lau-dá-ti-o. A-men.

(¶C) This is the *fa* clef. *Fa* is on the third line. Sing the syllables.

English translation for "Tantum Ergo":

Therefore, before this great Sacrament,
Let us bend low in adoration!
Let the Old Law
Give way to the New Rite.
Let faith supply
Where the senses fail!

To the Father and the Son
Praise and song of joy,
Together with salvation, honor,
Power, and blessing!
And to Him Who proceeds from Both
Equal be the praise!

America

SAMUEL FRANCIS SMITH

TRADITIONAL

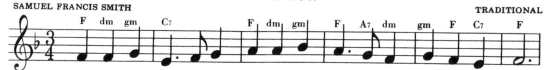

1. My coun-try, 'tis of thee, Sweet land of lib-er-ty, Of thee I sing.
2. My na-tive coun-try, thee, Land of the no-ble free, Thy name I love.
3. Let mu-sic swell the breeze, And ring from all the trees Sweet free-dom's song.
4. Our fa-thers' God! to Thee, Au-thor of lib-er-ty, To Thee we sing.

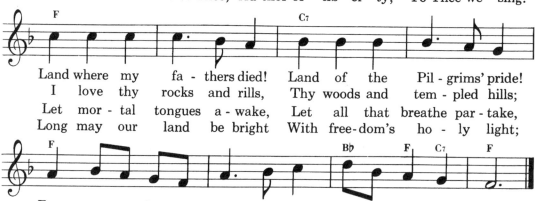

Land where my fa-thers died! Land of the Pil-grims' pride!
I love thy rocks and rills, Thy woods and tem-pled hills;
Let mor-tal tongues a-wake, Let all that breathe par-take,
Long may our land be bright With free-dom's ho-ly light;

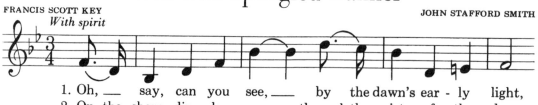

From ev-'ry__ moun-tain-side Let__ free-dom ring!
My heart__ with__ rap-ture thrills Like__ that a-bove.
Let rocks__ their__ si-lence break, The__ song pro-long.
Pro-tect__ us__ by Thy might, Great__ God our King!

The Star-Spangled Banner

FRANCIS SCOTT KEY

JOHN STAFFORD SMITH

With spirit

1. Oh, __ say, can you see, __ by the dawn's ear-ly light,
2. On the shore, dim-ly seen __ through the mists of the deep,
3. Oh, __ thus be it ev-er when __ free-men shall stand

What so proud-ly we hailed at the twi-light's last gleam-ing,
Where the foe's haught-y host in dread si-lence re-pos-es,
Be-tween their loved homes and the war's des-o-la-tion!

Whose broad stripes and bright stars, through the per - il - ous fight,
What is that which the breeze, o'er the tow - er - ing steep,
Blest with vic - t'ry and peace, may the heav'n-res - cued land

O'er the ram - parts we watched were so gal - lant - ly stream-ing?
As it fit - ful - ly blows, half con - ceals, half dis - clos - es?
Praise the Pow'r that hath made and pre - served us a na - tion!

And the rock - ets' red glare, the bombs burst - ing in air,
Now it catch - es the gleam of the morn - ing's first beam,
Then con - quer we must, when our cause it is just,

Gave proof through the night that our flag was still there.
In full glo - ry re - flect - ed, now shines on the stream.
And this be our mot - to: "In God is our trust!"

Oh, say, does that Star-Span-gled Ban - ner yet wave
'Tis the Star-Span - gled Ban - ner, oh, long may it wave
And the Star-Span - gled Ban - ner in tri - umph shall wave

O'er the land of the free and the home of the brave?
O'er the land of the free and the home of the brave!
O'er the land of the free and the home of the brave!

Lent and Passiontide

Create in me a clean heart, O God, and renew a right spirit within me.

Attende Domine

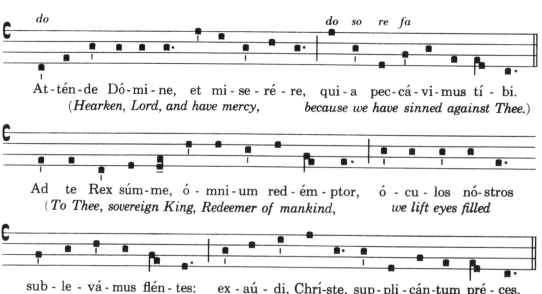

At-tén-de Dó-mi-ne, et mi-se-ré-re, qui-a pec-cá-vi-mus tí-bi.
(Hearken, Lord, and have mercy,   because we have sinned against Thee.)

Ad te Rex súm-me, ó-mni-um red-ém-ptor, ó-cu-los nó-stros
(To Thee, sovereign King, Redeemer of mankind,   we lift eyes filled

sub-le-vá-mus flén-tes: ex-aú-di, Chrí-ste, sup-pli-cán-tum pré-ces.
with tears:)   (Hear, O Christ, and answer the prayers of Thy suppliants.)

52

Stabat Mater

GIUSEPPE TARTINI
Arranged

1. Stá - bat__ Má - ter do - lo - ró - sa Jux - ta__
3. O quam trí - stis et af - flí - cta Fú - it__

crú - cem la - cri - mó - sa, Dum pen - dé - bat__
íl - la be - ne - dí - cta Má - ter__ U - ni -

Fine *Free rhythm*

Fí - li - us.
gé - ni - ti!

2. Cú - jus á - ni - mam ge - mén - tem,

D.C. al Fine

Con - tri - stá - tam et do - lén - tem Per - tran - sí - vit glá - di - us.

Remember that cut time (¢), which is actually 2/2 time, means that the half note is the unit of beat. Sing the hymn with two slow beats to a measure. The stanza in chant, of course, is in free rhythm.

Sleep, My Lovely

WELSH SLUMBER SONG

1. Sleep, my love - ly, in my arms, As soft and co-zy as a nest;
2. Sooth-ing calm to - night shall bless you, Ten - der slum-ber, sweet and deep;

I shall keep you close be-side me, You, the one I love the best.
Why, my loved one, are you smil-ing, Smil - ing sweet-ly in your sleep?

Harm shall nev-er touch you, dear one, Nor dis-turb your qui - et rest.
Are the heav'n-ly an - gels smil-ing, Smil - ing on you in your rest?

Hush - a - lu - la, hush - a - lu - la, Hush - a - lu - la, lu - la - lu.

Hush - a - lu - la, hush - a - lu - la, Hush - a - lu - la, lu - la - lu.

Clap this rhythm pattern: (♩. ♪♪♩).
Be sure not to confuse it with this rhythm pattern: (♩. ♪ ♩).

Prayer of the Norwegian Child
(Evening Prayer)

OLAF TROJORSON

SISTER JOHN JOSEPH, C.S.J.

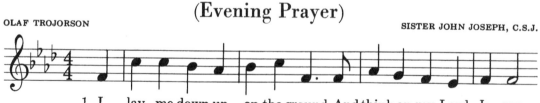

1. I lay me down up - on the ground, And think on my Lord Je - sus,
2. I rest my head up - on my bed, And think on my Lord Je - sus,

Each flow'r and tree tells me of Thee, And prais-es Thee, Lord Je-sus.
Send an-gels down to kneel a-round My bed at night, Lord Je-sus.

CHORUS

Lord Je-sus, think on me, Make my soul like un-to Thee,

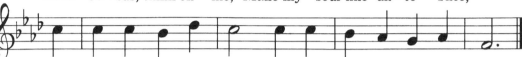

Lord Je-sus, think on me, Make my soul like un-to Thee.

Is this song in a major or a minor key?

Nobody Knows the Trouble I've Seen

NEGRO SPIRITUAL

No-bod-y knows the trou-ble I've seen, No-bod-y knows but Je-sus.

Fine

No-bod-y knows the trou-ble I've seen, Glo-ry hal-le-lu-ia.

1. Some-times I'm up, some-times I'm down, Oh, yes, Lord, Some-
2. Al-though you see me goin' long so, Oh, yes, Lord, I

D.C. al Fine

times I'm al-most to the ground, Oh, yes, ___ Lord.
have my tri-als here be-low, ___ Oh, yes, ___ Lord.

In spirituals you will often find syncopated rhythm. Where does it occur in this song?

Joseph, Our Hope

JULIA DERLETH

Jo-seph, our cer-tain hope be - low, Glo-ry of earth and heav'n, The

pil - lar of — the world art thou, To thee be praise im-mor-tal giv'n.

2. Thee as salvation's minister, The mighty Maker chose:
As foster father of the Word And as Mary's spotless spouse.

3. Lord of Lords and King of Kings, Ruler of sky and sea,
Whom heav'n and earth and hell obey: He was subject unto thee.

Sanctus

MASS XV

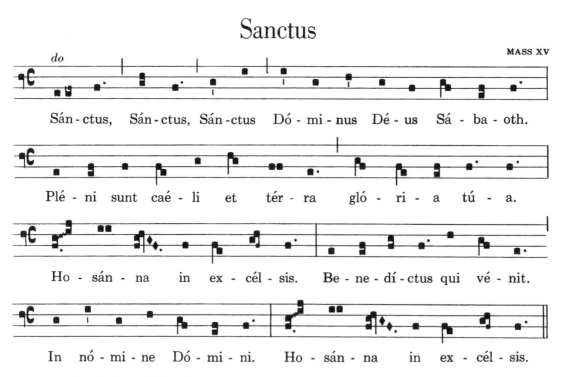

do

Sán - ctus, Sán - ctus, Sán - ctus Dó - mi - nus Dé - us Sá - ba - oth.

Plé - ni sunt caé - li et tér - ra gló - ri - a tú - a.

Ho - sán - na in ex - cél - sis. Be - ne - dí - ctus qui vé - nit.

In nó - mi - ne Dó - mi - ni. Ho - sán - na in ex - cél - sis.

On the first syllable of "Hosanna" there is a jagged note, called a *quilisma* (〰).
The note before it is lengthened slightly. Notice how the tones of this neum move
up the scale: re-mi-fa-so-la.

To Our Lady

A-ve, A-ve Ma-ri - a, gra-ti-a ple-na o - ra pro no - bis.

A-ve, A-ve Ma-ri - a, o - ra pro no - bis.

Ave Maria

A - ve Ma - rí - a, grá - ti - a, plé - na, Dó - mi - nus té - cum,

be - ne - dí - cta tu in mu - li - é - ri - bus, et be - ne - dí - ctus,

frú - ctus vén - tris tú - i, Jé - sus. Sán - cta Ma - rí - a, Má - ter Dé - i,

ó - ra pro nó - bis pec - ca - tó - ri - bus, nunc et in hó - ra mór - tis nó - strae. A - men.

This is a *salicus* group: (𝅘𝅥). The note with the ictus is slightly prolonged and the two highest notes are sung lightly. Notice the *pressus* in the last phrase.

America, the Beautiful

KATHARINE LEE BATES

SAMUEL A. WARD

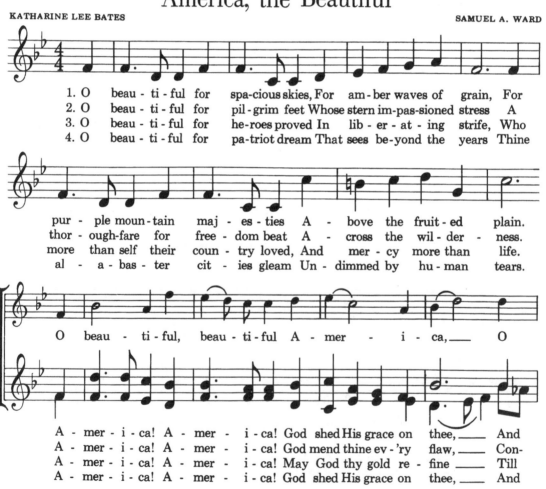

1. O beau-ti-ful for spa-cious skies, For am-ber waves of grain, For
2. O beau-ti-ful for pil-grim feet Whose stern im-pas-sioned stress A
3. O beau-ti-ful for he-roes proved In lib-er-at-ing strife, Who
4. O beau-ti-ful for pa-triot dream That sees be-yond the years Thine

pur-ple moun-tain maj-es-ties A-bove the fruit-ed plain.
thor-ough-fare for free-dom beat A-cross the wil-der-ness.
more than self their coun-try loved, And mer-cy more than life.
al-a-bas-ter cit-ies gleam Un-dimmed by hu-man tears.

O beau-ti-ful, beau-ti-ful A-mer-i-ca,___ O

A-mer-i-ca! A-mer-i-ca! God shed His grace on thee,___ And
A-mer-i-ca! A-mer-i-ca! God mend thine ev-'ry flaw,___ Con-
A-mer-i-ca! A-mer-i-ca! May God thy gold re-fine___ Till
A-mer-i-ca! A-mer-i-ca! God shed His grace on thee,___ And

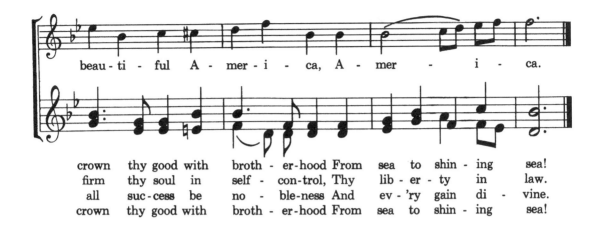

beau - ti - ful A - mer - i - ca, A - mer - i - ca.

crown	thy good with	broth - er-hood From	sea to shin - ing	sea!
firm	thy soul in	self - con-trol, Thy	lib - er - ty in	law.
all	suc - cess be	no - ble-ness And	ev - 'ry gain di - vine.
crown	thy good with	broth - er-hood From	sea to shin - ing	sea!

All Glory, Praise, and Honor

ST. THEODULPH
Translated by JOHN MASON NEALE

MELCHIOR TESCHNER

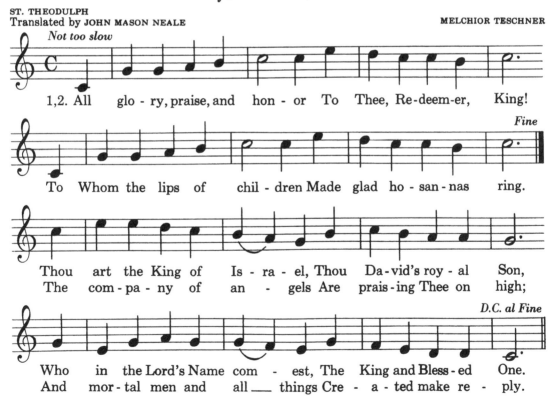

Not too slow

1,2. All glo - ry, praise, and hon - or To Thee, Re-deem-er, King!

Fine

To Whom the lips of chil - dren Made glad ho - san - nas ring.

Thou art the King of Is - ra - el, Thou Da - vid's roy - al Son,
The com - pa - ny of an - gels Are prais - ing Thee on high;

D.C. al Fine

Who in the Lord's Name com - est, The King and Bless - ed One.
And mor - tal men and all — things Cre - a - ted make re - ply.

What major key has no sharps or flats?

God so loved the world, as to give His only begotten Son.
John 3:16

O Sacred Head

13th CENTURY

H. HASSLER

1. O Sa - cred Head sur - round - ed By crown of pierc - ing thorn!
2. In this, Thy bit - ter pas - sion, Good Shep - herd, think of me,

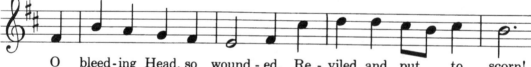

O bleed - ing Head, so wound - ed, Re - viled and put__ to scorn!
With Thy most sweet com - pas - sion, Un - wor - thy though I be:

Death's pal - lid hue comes o'er Thee, The glow of life de - cays,
Be - neath Thy cross a - bid - ing For - ev - er would I rest,

Yet an - gel hosts a - dore Thee, And trem - ble as they gaze.
In Thy dear love con - fid - ing, And with Thy pres - ence blest.

J. S. Bach made this melody famous by his beautiful harmonizations.

60

Hosanna Filio David

Ho-sán-na fí-li-o Dá-vid; be-ne-dí-ctus qui vé-nit
(Hosanna to the Son of David;   *blessed is He Who cometh*

in nó-mi-ne Dó-mi-ni. Rex Is-ra - el: Ho-sán-na in ex-cél-sis.
in the name of the Lord.)   *(King of Israel:*   *Hosanna in the highest.)*

Pueri Hebraeorum

Pu-e-ri He-brae-ó-rum, por-tán-tes rá-mos o-li-vá-rum,
(The children of the Hebrews,   *carrying olive branches,)*

ob-vi-a-vé-runt Dó-mi-no, cla-mán-tes, et di-cén-tes:
(Came to meet our Lord,   *crying out and saying:*

Ho-sán-na in ex-cél-sis.
Hosanna in the highest!)

In this chant there is a *pressus* on "clamantes."
There is also a *pressus* on "dicentes."
Can you find them?

61

Eastertide

l - le - lú - ia,   al - le - lú - ia,   al - le - lú - ia.

Easter Hymn

1. Al - le - lu - ia, ___ Christ the Lord is ris'n on high, al - le - lu - ia.
2. Al - le - lu - ia, ___ To God the Fa-ther let us sing, al - le - lu - ia.
3. Al - le - lu - ia, ___ Hymns of glo - ry, songs of praise, al - le - lu - ia.
4. Al - le - lu - ia, ___ Risen Lord   all praise to Thee, al - le - lu - ia.

Now He   lives no more to die, Al - le - lu - ia, al - le - lu - ia.
To God the Son our Ris - en King, Al - le - lu - ia, al - le - lu - ia.
Father   un - to Thee we raise, Al - le - lu - ia, al - le - lu - ia.
Ever   with the Spir - it be. Al - le - lu - ia, al - le - lu - ia.

An angel of the Lord descended from heaven and said to the women:
He Whom you seek is risen as He said, alleluia.

Alleluia

WOLFGANG AMADEUS MOZART

Al - le - lu - ia, al - le - lu - ia, ___ Al - le - lu - ia, al - le - lu - ia.

Al - le - lu - ia, al - le - lu - ia, ___ Al - le - lu - ia, al - le - lu - ia.

Christ the Lord Has Risen

TWELFTH CENTURY HYMN

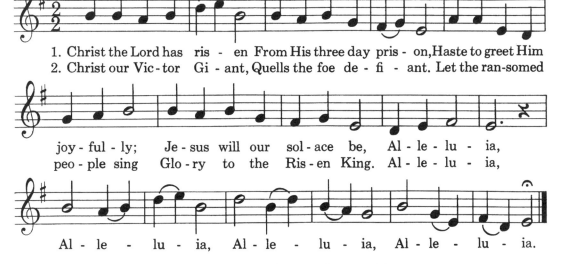

1. Christ the Lord has ris - en From His three day pris - on, Haste to greet Him
2. Christ our Vic - tor Gi - ant, Quells the foe de - fi - ant. Let the ran-somed

joy - ful - ly; Je - sus will our sol - ace be, Al - le - lu - ia,
peo - ple sing Glo - ry to the Ris - en King. Al - le - lu - ia,

Al - le - lu - ia, Al - le - lu - ia, Al - le - lu - ia.

In this hymn the half note is the unit of beat.

63

Alleluia, Christ Is Risen!

SISTER CECILIA, S.C.

Al - le - lu - ia, al - le - lu - ia, Al - le - lu - ia, al-le-lu - ia!

Christ is — ris-en — from the — dead, Christ is — ris-en — as He said.

A canon is a song for two or more voices in which all sing the same melody, but begin at different times. The first voice is called the "leader", the second voice is the "follower"

Adoremus and Laudate

Ad - o - ré - mus in ae - tér-num Sanctíssimum Sa - cra - mén-tum.

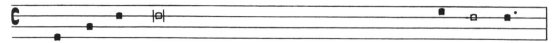

Ps. 1. Lau-dá - te Dóminum ómnes gén - tes:
2. Quóniam confirmáta est super nos misericórdia é - jus:
3. Glória Pátri, et Fí - li - o,
4. Sicut érat in princípio, et nunc, et sém - per,

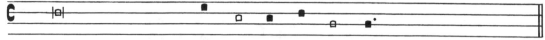

laudáte éum ó - mnes pó - pu - li.
et véritas Dómini mánet in ae - tér - num.
et Spi - rí - tu - i Sán - cto.
et in saécula saecu - ló - rum. A - men. *(Repeat Adorémus)*

If you be risen with Christ, seek the things that are above, where Christ is sitting at the right hand of God, alleluia.

Bells Are Ringing

FRENCH MELODY

Bells are ring-ing al - le - lu - ia! Christ is ris - en from the

dead; An-gels sing-ing al - le - lu - ia! Christ is liv-ing, as He

said. Let us join their glad re - joic-ing, His tri - um-phant glo-ry

voic-ing, And each heart its hom-age pay To our Sav-iour, al - le -

This song is in f minor. Which major key has the same signature?

lu - ia, Sing-ing this fair East-er day!

65

At the Gate of Heaven

MEXICAN FOLK SONG
Arranged by D.Y.G.

1. At the gate of Heav'n lit-tle shoes___ they are sell-ing,
For the lit-tle bare-foot-ed an-gels there dwell-ing,
2. God will bless the chil-dren so peace-ful-ly sleep-ing,
God will bless the moth-ers whose love___ they are keep-ing.

DESCANT

Slum-ber, my ba-by,___ slum-ber a-rru, a-rru.

Slum-ber now, my ba-by, a-rru, a-rru.

Jesu, Joy of Man's Desiring

CHORAL from CANTATA NO. 147
JOHANN SEBASTIAN BACH

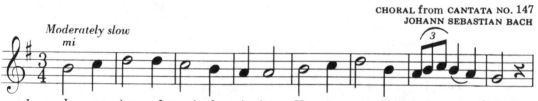

Moderately slow

1. Je-su, joy of man's de-sir-ing, Ho-ly wis-dom, love___ most bright,
2. Through the way where hope is guid-ing, Hark, what peace-ful mu-sic___ rings!

Drawn by Thee, our souls as-pir-ing Soar to un-cre-a-ted light.
Where the flocks in Thee con-fid-ing Drink of joy from death-less springs.

Word of God, our flesh that fash-ioned With the fire of life im-pas-sioned,
Theirs is beau-ty's fair-est pleas-ure, Theirs is wis-dom's ho-liest treas-ure.

Striv-ing still to truth un-known, Soar-ing, sing-ing round Thy throne.
Thou dost ev-er lead Thine own, In the love of joy un-known.

Listen to a good recording of "Jesu, Joy of Man's Desiring."

Sing the triplets (♪♪♪) evenly on one beat.

Agnus Dei

MASS XV

A-gnus Dé-i, qui tól-lis pec-cá-ta mún-di: mi-se-ré-re nó-bis.

A-gnus Dé-i, qui tól-lis pec-cá-ta mún-di: mi-se-ré-re nó-bis.

A-gnus Dé-i, qui tól-lis pec-cá-ta mún-di: dó-na nó-bis pá-cem.

The neum above Dei ( ) in the first line is called a *porrectus*. The syllable names are *re, do, mi*.

Pentecost

Grant, we beseech Thee, almighty and merciful God, that the Holy Ghost coming to us may make us the temple of His Glory by dwelling in us.

Come, Holy Spirit

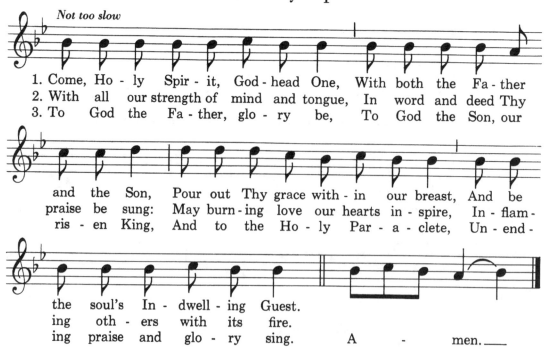

Not too slow

1. Come, Ho - ly Spir - it, God - head One, With both the Fa - ther and the Son, Pour out Thy grace with - in our breast, And be the soul's In - dwell - ing Guest.

2. With all our strength of mind and tongue, In word and deed Thy praise be sung: May burn - ing love our hearts in - spire, In - flam - ing oth - ers with its fire.

3. To God the Fa - ther, glo - ry be, To God the Son, our ris - en King, And to the Ho - ly Par - a - clete, Un - end - ing praise and glo - ry sing. A - men.

Benediction and glory, and wisdom, and thanksgiving, honor, power, and strength, to our God for ever and ever.

The Doxology

Arranged by
MOST REV. AMBROSE SENYSHEN, O.S.B.M.
APOSTOLIC EXARCH of STAMFORD

From the BYZANTINE LITURGY

Sla - va Ot - tsu, i Si - nu, i Svya - to - mu Du - khu,

i ni - nee i pris - no, i - vo vee - ki vee-kov, A - min.

Ukrainian Catholics sing the *Gloria Patri* in this way at Holy Mass. You might like to try singing the original Slavonic words of this hymn. Pronounce *i* as in *giver*, other vowels and consonants as in English. If you wish to sing *The Doxology* in English, use the rhythmic arrangement below.

Glo-ry be — to the Fa-ther, and to the Son, and to the Ho - ly Ghost.

And now and ev - er, and un-to a - ges of a - ges, A - men.

69

O God, the Author of all things, Who established the law of labor for the human race, graciously grant, that by the example and patronage of St. Joseph, we may accomplish the works which You have commanded and obtain the reward which You have promised.

Collect: Feast of Saint Joseph, the Workman.

Great St. Joseph

SISTER JOHN JOSEPH, C.S.J.

1. Great St. Jo-seph, son of Da-vid, Fos-ter fa-ther of our Lord,
2. All who toil and all who la-bor Find their help and strength in thee.

Spouse of Ma-ry, ev-er Vir-gin, Keep-ing o'er them watch and word.
All in need and all in sor-row, Thou wilt their pro-tec-tor be.

In the sta-ble thou didst guard them With a fa-ther's lov-ing care;
When our day of life is clos-ing, Guard us with a fa-ther's love;

Thou by God's com-mand didst save them From the cru-el Her-od's snare.
Keep us safe from fear and sor-row, Lead us to our home a-bove.

Chant for the Feast of the Ascension

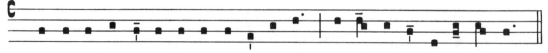

A-scén-dit Dé-us in ju-bi-la-ti-ó-ne: Al-le-lú-ia, al-le-lú-ia.
(God ascended with jubilee:) *(Al-le-lu-ia, al-le-lu-ia.)*

70

Et Dó-mi-nus in vó-ce tú-bae. Gló-ri-a Pá-tri, et Fí-li-o,
(And the Lord with the sound of a trumpet.)

et Spi-rí-tu-i Sán-cto. A-scén-dit Dé-us in ju-bi-la-ti-ó-ne:

Al-le-lú-ia, al-le-lú-ia.

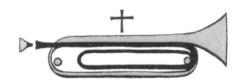

Lord Have Mercy

Arranged by
MOST REV. AMBROSE SENYSHEN, O.S.B.M.
APOSTOLIC EXARCH of STAMFORD

From the **BYZANTINE LITURGY**

Ho-spo-di, po-mi-luy. Ho-spo-di, po-mi-luy.
Lord have mer-cy. Lord have mer-cy.

Ho-spo-di, po-mi-luy. Ho-spo-di, po-mi-luy.
Lord have mer-cy. Lord have mer-cy.

The prayer *Hospodi Pomiluy* occurs in Byzantine Liturgy as *Kyrie Eleison* does in the Latin Liturgy. The original Greek, which is still used in the Latin Rite, was translated into the ancient Slavonic language. This language is still used in the Byzantine Rite.

The Holy Sacrifice of the Mass is identical in all Catholic Churches, but the prayers and ceremonies which surround the central act of Sacrifice may differ somewhat in their form and sequence.

We call these various ceremonies a Liturgy or Rite.

Many American Catholics belong to the Byzantine Rite. Their prayers and ceremonies at Mass are very ancient and very beautiful. Perhaps you can find an opportunity to assist at Mass in a Byzantine Church.

When you wish to sing this hymn in English, notice how the notes are tied to alter the rhythm.

We Crown Our Lady

(A May Crowning Ceremony)

ALL. In the Name of the Father, and of the Son, and of the Holy Spirit. Amen.

SOLO VOICE. Hail Mary, full of grace, the Lord is with thee, blessed art thou among women, and blessed is the fruit of thy womb, Jesus.

ALL. Holy Mary, Mother of God, pray for us sinners now and at the hour of our death. Amen.

SOLO VOICE. Let us give honor to the Virgin Mary, who was conceived without sin.

ALL. Virgin most powerful, pray for us.
Virgin most faithful, pray for us.
Virgin most merciful, pray for us.

Hail, Mary, Full of Grace

TRADITIONAL

1. Hail, Ma - ry, full of grace, pure flow'r of Ad - am's race, Moth - er of
2. Foun - tain of all our joy, wis - dom with - out al - loy, Ves - sel of

Christ the Lord, Heav - en - ly Queen. **CHORUS** Maid - en most beau - ti - ful,
hon - or true, and heav'n-ly grace.

Vir - gin most pow - er - ful, Moth - er most mer - ci - ful, hear us, we pray.

Show us thy lov - ing and moth - er - ly care.

SOLO VOICE. Let us give honor to the Virgin Mary, who gave birth to the Son of the Eternal Father.

ALL. Mother of Christ, pray for us.
Mother of Divine Grace, pray for us.
Mother of Our Redeemer, pray for us.

Virgin Wholly Marvelous

FOURTH CENTURY

TRADITIONAL

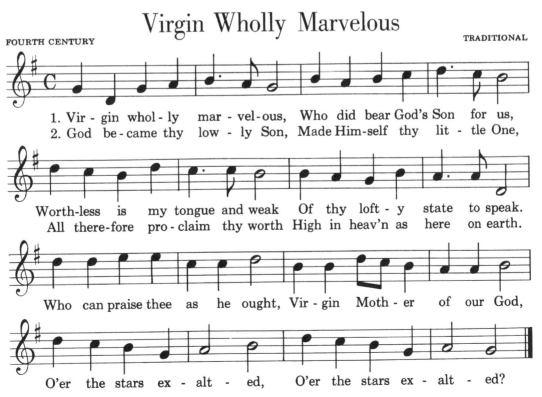

1. Vir-gin whol-ly mar-vel-ous, Who did bear God's Son for us,
2. God be-came thy low-ly Son, Made Him-self thy lit-tle One,

Worth-less is my tongue and weak Of thy loft-y state to speak.
All there-fore pro-claim thy worth High in heav'n as here on earth.

Who can praise thee as he ought, Vir-gin Moth-er of our God,

O'er the stars ex-alt-ed, O'er the stars ex-alt-ed?

Solo Voice. Let us give honor to the Virgin Mary, who is Queen of
heaven and earth.
All. Queen of angels, pray for us.
Queen of all saints, pray for us.
Queen assumed into heaven, pray for us.
Queen of peace, pray for us.

O Queen of Heavenly Majesty

TRADITIONAL

1. O Queen of heav'n-ly maj - es - ty, Ma - ri - a!
2. Thee, gen - tle Moth-er, we im-plore, Ma - ri - a!

Thou glo-rious Queen of vic - to - ry, Ma - ri - a!
For us thou wert af - flict - ed sore, Ma - ri - a!

All to thee sub - ject - ed lies, e'en the foe who thee de - fies.
Let not all thy bit - ter pain for us sin - ners be in vain.

Oh, help us strug - gle, and lead in bat - tle, In
Oh, help us strug - gle, and lead in bat - tle, In

death and life, in ev - 'ry strife, Ma - ri - a!
death and life, in ev - 'ry strife, Ma - ri - a!

Solo Voice. O Blessed Virgin Mary, Mother of God, and Queen of
heaven, we choose thee this day for our Queen and Mother.
(A girl or boy places the crown upon the statue of Our Lady.)

74

Hail, Holy Queen, Enthroned Above

TRADITIONAL

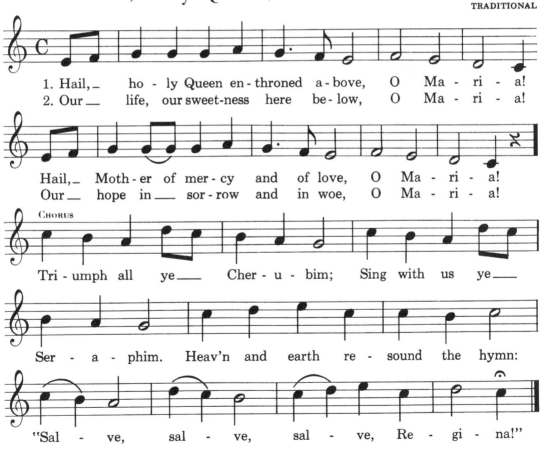

1. Hail, — ho - ly Queen en - throned a - bove, O Ma - ri - a!
2. Our — life, our sweet-ness here be - low, O Ma - ri - a!

Hail, — Moth - er of mer - cy and of love, O Ma - ri - a!
Our — hope in — sor - row and in woe, O Ma - ri - a!

CHORUS

Tri - umph all ye — Cher - u - bim; Sing with us ye —

Ser - a - phim. Heav'n and earth re - sound the hymn:

"Sal - ve, sal - ve, sal - ve, Re - gi - na!"

THE END

75

Blessed be the Holy Trinity and undivided Unity; we will give glory to Him because He has shown His mercy to us.

Blessed Trinity
(Two-part Canon)

S. J. J.

THOMAS TALLIS

All praise and glo - ry be to Thee, O un - di - vid - ed

All praise and glo - ry be to Thee, O

Trin - i - ty! Our lov - ing Fa - ther, bless - ed Son, And

un - di - vid - ed Trin - i - ty! Our lov - ing Fa - ther,

Ho - ly Spir - it, Three in One.

bless - ed Son, And Ho - ly Spir - it, Three in One.

Sing this canon in a dignified, reverent manner.

O God, Who cannot change or fail,
Guiding the hours as they roll by,
Brightening with beams the morning pale,
And burning in the midday sky,

Quench Thou the fires of hate and strife,
The wasting fever of the heart;
From perils guard our feeble life,
And to our souls Thy peace impart.

From the Divine Office

The Holy Trinity

R. KNOX

BAYEUX MELODY

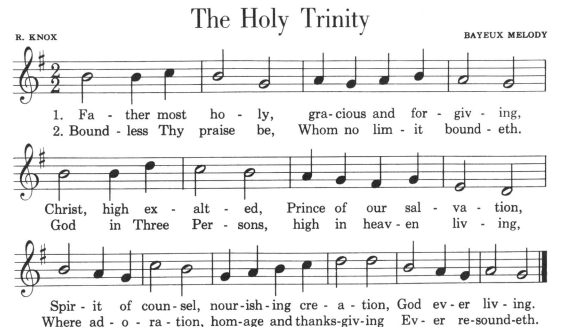

1. Fa - ther most ho - ly, gra - cious and for - giv - ing,
2. Bound - less Thy praise be, Whom no lim - it bound - eth.

Christ, high ex - alt - ed, Prince of our sal - va - tion,
God in Three Per - sons, high in heav - en liv - ing,

Spir - it of coun - sel, nour - ish - ing cre - a - tion, God ev - er liv - ing.
Where ad - o - ra - tion, hom - age and thanks - giv - ing Ev - er re - sound - eth.

How many beats are there in a measure?
What is the unit of beat?

Cor Jesu

Cor Je - su Sa - cra - tís - si - mum, mi - se - ré - re no - bis.
(*Most Sacred Heart of Jesus,   have mercy on us.*)

Can you find three counts in an arsis and in a thesis in this chant?

Cor, Arca Legem Continens

TRADITIONAL

1. Cor, ar - ca le - gem cón - ti - nens, Non ser - vi - tú - tis vé - te - ris, Sed
2. Te vul - ne - rá - tum cá - ri - tas, I - ctu pa - tén - ti vó - lu - it, A-

grá - ti - ae, sed vé - ni - ae, Sed et mi - se - ri - cór - di - ae.
mó - ris in - vi - sí - bi - lis, Ut ve - ne - ré - mur vúl - ne - ra.

O Heart, ark containing the law, not of the ancient
servitude, but of grace, of pardon and of mercy.

Your charity wished that, being wounded by a visible
blow, we might venerate the wounds of Your invisible
Love.

Hymn to the Sacred Heart

O Thou, the Son of God most high, Thou Fa-ther of the life to be,
Lord, keep us ev-er in Thy heart, Thy ten-der love to feel and know,

O Prince of Peace, to Thee we cry, We bring our song of praise to Thee.
The joys of heav'n to us im-part, When we shall leave these walks be-low.

The Mother

CHRISTINE TURNER CURTIS

EDVARD GRIEG

1. The moth-er is the bea-con light of ev-'ry house and home.__ To
2. The moth-er is the com-fort-er in sor-row and in fear. __ She

all her chil-dren near and far, The moth-er is __ the
takes our part when things go wrong, Her love __ is al-ways

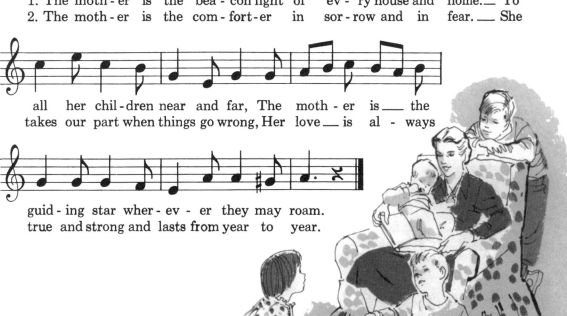

guid-ing star wher-ev-er they may roam.
true and strong and lasts from year to year.

Evensong

LYNN SEELEY

SELIM PALMGREN

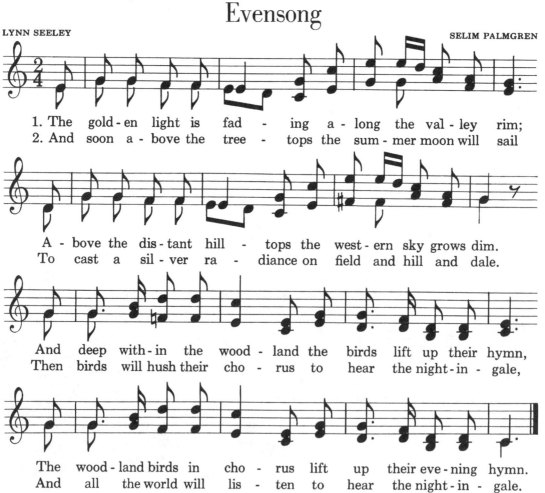

1. The gold-en light is fad - ing a - long the val - ley rim;
2. And soon a - bove the tree - tops the sum - mer moon will sail

A - bove the dis - tant hill - tops the west - ern sky grows dim.
To cast a sil - ver ra - diance on field and hill and dale.

And deep with - in the wood - land the birds lift up their hymn,
Then birds will hush their cho - rus to hear the night - in - gale,

The wood - land birds in cho - rus lift up their eve - ning hymn.
And all the world will lis - ten to hear the night - in - gale.

What does the time signature mean? What is the key?
Find the tonic chord, C-E-G-C, on the keyboard.

Memorial Day

CHRISTINE CANEVIN

LUDWIG VAN BEETHOVEN

1. Far, far a - way we hear the bu - gles call - ing:
2. Shin - ing and clear, the dis - tant stars are gleam - ing;

O - ver the land the qui - et night is fall - ing.
Furled is the flag no long - er proud - ly stream - ing.

Sol - diers rest in peace and glo - ry, all their bat - tles now are won,
Where the sol - diers sleep in hon - or sounds of drums and bu - gles cease.

As a na - tion hon - ors ev - 'ry loy - al ___ son. ___
God, Who gave them cour - age, give them now Thy ___ peace! ___

As you sing, be careful to distinguish between evenly and unevenly divided beats.

81

Columbia, the Gem of the Ocean

THOMAS à BECKET

1. O Co-lum-bia, the gem of the o-cean, The home of the brave and the free, —

The shrine of each pa-triot's de - vo-tion, A world of-fers hom-age to thee.

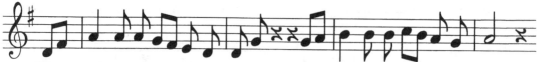

Thy man-dates make he-roes as - sem-ble, When lib - er-ty's form stands in view;

Thy ban-ners make ty - ran-ny trem-ble When borne by the red, white and blue;

82

CHORUS

When borne by the red, white and blue, When borne by the red, white and blue.

Thy ban-ners make tyr - an-ny trem-ble, When borne by the red, white and blue.

2. When war wing'd its wide desolation,
   And threatened the land to deform,
   The ark then of freedom's foundation,
   Columbia rode safe through the storm:
   With her garlands of vict'ry around her,
   When so proudly she bore her bold crew,
   With her flag proudly floating before her,
   The boast of the red, white and blue.

CHORUS

   The boast of the red, white and blue,
   The boast of the red, white and blue,
   With her flag proudly floating before her,
   The boast of the red, white and blue.

3. The Star-spangled Banner bring hither,
   O'er Columbia's true sons let it wave;
   May the wreath they have won never wither,
   Nor its stars cease to shine on the brave.
   May the service united ne'er sever,
   But hold to their colors so true;
   The army and navy forever,
   Three cheers for the red, white and blue.

CHORUS

   Three cheers for the red, white and blue,
   Three cheers for the red, white and blue,
   The army and navy forever,
   Three cheers for the red, white and blue.

83

The Good King
(A Story of the Crusades)

The Players

NARRATOR
SIR DENIS } Knights
SIR LAURENT
JEAN } Pages
PIERRE
ARMAND—A Troubadour

PÈRE CHRISTOPHE } Chaplains
PÈRE RENE
LOUIS IX, KING OF FRANCE
CHORUS OF CRUSADERS—Boys
CHORUS OF HOLY MARTYRS—Girls

(*No stage setting is necessary. The* CRUSADERS *wear a white tunic with a red cross on the breast, and the Crusader's hood. The* KNIGHTS *should have shields and swords. The* PAGES *wear hose and doublet, the* CHAPLAINS, *cassocks and very long surplices. The* KING *wears a simple gold crown over his hood. The* HOLY MARTYRS *wear long, pastel-colored gowns and carry palm branches.*)

Scene 1.

NARRATOR. Many centuries ago the kings and nobles of Europe went to war to save the Holy Land from the hands of the infidels. They bore many hardships and fought bravely under the standard of the Cross. At first successful, they soon fell victim to the fevers and plagues of the East, and the Saracens again took the Holy Land.

Among the Crusaders there was one who was a great saint, Louis IX, King of France. A good man, just and holy, a true father to his people, a loyal son of the Holy Church, Louis of France tried twice to set free the Holy City of Jerusalem. Both times he failed. He never saw the Holy Land.

This is a story of his last Crusade. The scene is in France, where the Crusaders are preparing to take ships to the Holy Land.

(SIR DENIS, SIR LAURENT, *the* PAGES, ARMAND, *and a group of* CRUSADERS *are sitting by the roadside.* SIR DENIS *is telling a story of the Crusade.*)

SIR DENIS. Never did mortal man fight as bravely as our king when we defeated the Saracens at Damietta. That was a fierce battle. On all sides the infidels surrounded us. They blew their horns and beat upon their drums, and called upon Mohammed to help them. But the king led us on to victory, and we took the city.

JEAN. I wish I could have been there. I would have followed the king to victory or to death.

SIR LAURENT. Well, my boy, again the king leads us against the Saracens. Again we ride to deliver the Holy Land from the unbeliever, and this time you ride with us.

JEAN. But I am only a page. I cannot carry a sword or ride to battle.

SIR DENIS. Every knight must first be a page. He must bear himself nobly and bravely at all times. When he has learned all that a knight must know, he will receive the Accolade from our most gracious king and will become a knight.

ARMAND. Page or knight, marquis or king—all this matters little to me. I am only a poor troubadour, but when I sing everyone listens—even the king.

PIERRE. Sing us a song now, Armand. We have not had a song all day.

ARMAND. What shall I sing, a love song?

JEAN. No! a song of the Crusaders!

PIERRE. Sing a song of knights and pages, a song of men marching to the Holy Land.

ARMAND. (*Tuning his harp*). This is a song of a knight who rode away to the Crusades. He left a beautiful lady at home to wait for him.

There Was a Knight

S. C.

OLD FRENCH TUNE

1. There was a knight so— bold who loved a la-dy— fair.
2. She gave the knight a— ring, all made of gold so— fair.

He rode a-way to— war to save the Ho-ly— Land.
All set with ru-bies— red to show her love for— him.

He said, "My la-dy so— fair, oh pray, oh,
She said, "These ru-bies so— fair, will show my

pray for— me, Till I re-turn in— the spring-time."
love for— you, Till you re-turn in— the spring-time."

SIR LAURENT. That is a fine song, Armand, but very sad. Give us a
brave song. Give us the marching song of the Crusaders.
ARMAND. Sir, let the knights sing that song, and I will listen. It is the
song of men who march to war, and I am only a troubadour.
SIR LAURENT. Very well, we shall sing it for you.
(*The* CRUSADERS *sing* "Merciful Saviour")

Merciful Saviour

CRUSADERS' HYMN

1. Mer - ci - ful Sav - iour, King of Cre - a - tion, Tru - ly, ___
2. Mer - ci - ful Sav - iour, Lord of the Na - tions, Son of ___

God and ___ tru - ly Man! Je - sus we love ___ Thee,
God and ___ Son of Man! Glo - ry and hon - or,

Je - sus we serve Thee, Now and for e - ter - ni - ty.
praise, ad - o - ra - tion, Now and ev - er - more be Thine.

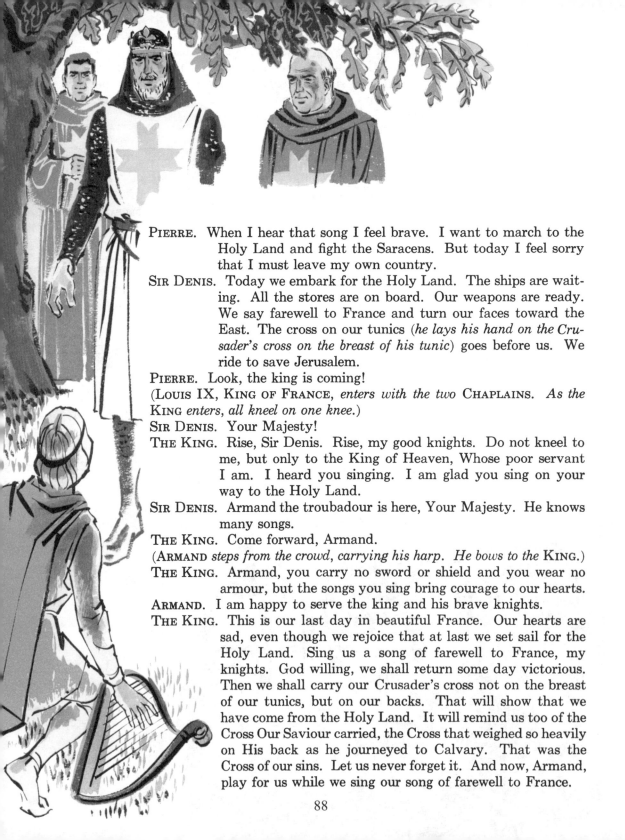

PIERRE. When I hear that song I feel brave. I want to march to the Holy Land and fight the Saracens. But today I feel sorry that I must leave my own country.

SIR DENIS. Today we embark for the Holy Land. The ships are waiting. All the stores are on board. Our weapons are ready. We say farewell to France and turn our faces toward the East. The cross on our tunics (*he lays his hand on the Crusader's cross on the breast of his tunic*) goes before us. We ride to save Jerusalem.

PIERRE. Look, the king is coming!

(LOUIS IX, KING OF FRANCE, *enters with the two* CHAPLAINS. *As the* KING *enters, all kneel on one knee.*)

SIR DENIS. Your Majesty!

THE KING. Rise, Sir Denis. Rise, my good knights. Do not kneel to me, but only to the King of Heaven, Whose poor servant I am. I heard you singing. I am glad you sing on your way to the Holy Land.

SIR DENIS. Armand the troubadour is here, Your Majesty. He knows many songs.

THE KING. Come forward, Armand.

(ARMAND *steps from the crowd, carrying his harp. He bows to the* KING.)

THE KING. Armand, you carry no sword or shield and you wear no armour, but the songs you sing bring courage to our hearts.

ARMAND. I am happy to serve the king and his brave knights.

THE KING. This is our last day in beautiful France. Our hearts are sad, even though we rejoice that at last we set sail for the Holy Land. Sing us a song of farewell to France, my knights. God willing, we shall return some day victorious. Then we shall carry our Crusader's cross not on the breast of our tunics, but on our backs. That will show that we have come from the Holy Land. It will remind us too of the Cross Our Saviour carried, the Cross that weighed so heavily on His back as he journeyed to Calvary. That was the Cross of our sins. Let us never forget it. And now, Armand, play for us while we sing our song of farewell to France.

Song of the Crusaders

SISTER CECILIA, S.C.

FRENCH PILGRIMAGE SONG

1. When all the fields were green with ear - ly grain, we rode a - way,
2. Soon will the win - ter winds be ech - o - ing our last fare - well,

When all the land was sweet with sum - mer rain, we rode a - way.
Shall we re - turn a - gain when spring re-turns? Oh, who can tell!

Now all the wheat and bar - ley fields gold with the har - vest stand,
This is our vow to fol - low Christ, go where the cross may lead,

Yet we go rid - ing on through love - ly France, on to the Ho - ly Land.
Pledg-ing our swords to save the Ho - ly Land, this is the ho - ly deed.

Scene 2.

NARRATOR. And so the Crusaders came to Africa, to the City of Tunis. There they landed and attacked the Saracens. It was a fierce battle, but the Crusaders were victorious. They drove the Saracens out into the desert and took the city. All fought bravely, but Louis the King was bravest of all.

(*The* CRUSADERS *enter, singing* "Merciful Saviour." *They break ranks, put down their shields. Some sit down on the ground, others stand talking in small groups.*)

SIR LAURENT. My friends, the City of Tunis is ours.

SIR DENIS. It is only our first victory on the way to Jerusalem.

PIERRE. The Saracens fought fiercely.

SIR DENIS. Very fiercely, my boy. Many of our brave knights were killed.

JEAN. They died fighting for the Holy Land. Surely Our Saviour has taken them to heaven.

SIR LAURENT. God grant it may be so. Tomorrow the chaplains will offer Masses for their souls. But now the wounded must be cared for.

JEAN. I can help.

PIERRE. And so can I.

SIR LAURENT. Good. Come with me to the hospital tents. There will be plenty of work for you.

JEAN. Look! The king!

(*The* KING *enters. All kneel, but rise at a sign from his hand.*)

THE KING. My good knights, you fought like Michael and his angels.

SIR LAURENT. Your Majesty, we only followed you. You were in the thick of the battle.

THE KING. That is where a king should be, Sir Laurent.

SIR DENIS. I feared for your safety, Your Majesty. The arrows of the Saracens fell like rain around you.

THE KING. If God wills that I die in battle, His Holy Will be done. I
pray that I may see Jerusalem, but His Holy Will be done.

PIERRE. Here comes Armand, the troubadour.

(ARMAND *enters, his harp slung over his shoulder.*)

THE KING. Well, my troubadour, can you sing a song of our victory?

ARMAND. I am making one, Your Majesty. It will soon be finished.

THE KING. Then let us sing a hymn in praise of Our Lady. She is
Queen of the Heavenly Jerusalem. She will lead us to the
Holy Land.

(*All sing "Hail, Queen of Heaven."*)

Hail, Queen of Heaven

ELEVENTH CENTURY HYMN

1. Hail, Queen of Heav - en, Vir - gin, Moth - er.
2. Hail, Star of O - cean, Vir - gin, Moth - er.

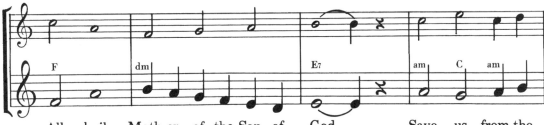

All hail, Moth-er of the Son of God.___ Save us from the
All hail, pur-est flow'r of Ad-am's race.___ Be thou our de-

E - vil One, we pray thee. Maid for-ev - er pure and sin - less.
fend-er as we jour-ney. Lead us to the light of heav - en.

Scene 3.

NARRATOR. After the landing at Tunis, the Crusaders laid siege to the City of Carthage. But the walls were strong and well defended. No Saracens came to fight the Crusaders, but a worse enemy besieged them: plague broke out in the camp. The knights were too weak to mount their horses, the archers could not draw their bows. Louis the King went from tent to tent encouraging his Crusaders, sometimes caring for them with his own hands.

(PIERRE *and* JEAN *enter. They carry shields over their shoulders. They sit down and begin to polish the shields.*)

PIERRE. Sir Laurent will soon be well again, please God. I shall have his shield ready for the battle with the Saracens.

JEAN. Listen, I hear Armand singing.

(ARMAND *enters, singing and playing on his harp.*)

To the Holy Land We Ride

TWELFTH CENTURY MELODY

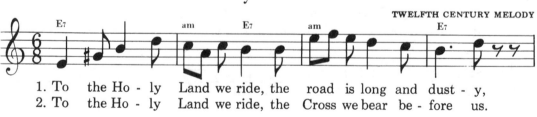

1. To the Ho - ly Land we ride, the road is long and dust - y,
2. To the Ho - ly Land we ride, the Cross we bear be - fore us.

All the way my harp I play, my harp so true and trust - y.
God to give the vic - to - ry, His saints to march be - fore us.

I sing my song as on our way we jour-ney.
I sing my song as on our way we jour-ney.

PIERRE. That is a new song, Armand.

ARMAND. Yes, I made it yesterday. I am going to sing it for the king.

JEAN. Teach it to us.

ARMAND. Not until the king has heard it.

PIERRE. We can help you sing it for him.

ARMAND. Very well; this is the way it goes.

(ARMAND *repeats the song. During it the* KING, PÈRE CHRISTOPHE, PÈRE RENE, *and* SIR DENIS *enter. They stand listening, not noticed by the boys and* ARMAND.)

THE KING (*Coming forward*). That is a good song, Armand. It pleases me.

ARMAND (*Bowing*). I made it only yesterday, Your Majesty.

THE KING. Go to the tent of Sir Laurent and sing it for him. He is weak and sad. Your song will cheer him.

(ARMAND *and the boys bow, go out.*)

THE KING. Sir Denis, the sickness grows worse.

SIR DENIS. Yes, Your Majesty. During the night fifty men died.

PÈRE RENE. This morning our Masses were offered for their souls.

THE KING. Our knights are dying of the fever. Carthage stands before us unconquerable. God tries us sorely. Oh, Jerusalem, shall we ever see thy holy places?

PÈRE CHRISTOPHE. Do not give up hope, Your Majesty. We shall reach the Holy Land.

THE KING. I am beginning to think otherwise, Père Christophe. Twice I have tried. Twice I have failed.

PÈRE CHRISTOPHE. It is in God's hands.

THE KING. Perhaps He wills that I die here, far from France, far from the Holy Land. But His Will be done.

PÈRE RENE. There is the Jerusalem that is above, the Holy City that St. John speaks of in the Apocalypse.

THE KING. To that city, indeed, we all journey. God willing, we shall again meet there those who have gone before us. Now leave me, my friends. It is my wish to pray alone.

(The others go out. The KING kneels, draws his sword and holds it before him, the cross hilt upward. The CHORUS OF HOLY MARTYRS enters singing "Crux Fidelis." After the hymn the KING rises, goes out.)

Crux Fidelis

Crux fi - dé - lis, __ in - ter ó - mnes Ar - bor ú - na __ nó - bi - lis:
Faith-ful cross, O __ tree all ho - ly, __ Tree all peer - less and di - vine:

Núl - la __ síl - va tá - lem pró - fert, Frón - de, fló - re, gér - mi - ne:
No grove, no for - est on earth can show Such leaf and flow - er as thine:

Dúl - ce __ lí - gnum, dul - ces clá - vos, Dúl - ce pón - dus sús - ti - net.
O sweet the nails and sweet the wood La - den with so sweet a load.

Scene 4.

NARRATOR. Before long the king himself fell victim to the plague. He lay tossing with fever in his tent, praying for the safety of his army, praying for his beloved France, which now he knew he would never see again. With great devotion he received the Last Sacraments and commended his soul to God.

(SIR DENIS *and a group of* KNIGHTS *enter, walking slowly.* PIERRE *and* JEAN *run to meet them.*)

PIERRE. Oh, Sir Denis, the king must not die!

SIR DENIS. My boy, we pray that he may not die, but God's Will be done.

PIERRE. But who will lead us to the Holy Land?

SIR DENIS. That, too, is in God's hands. Look, Armand is coming.

ARMAND. I have brought my harp to sing to the king.

SIR DENIS. They will not let you in the tent, Armand. Only the chaplains and the physicians are there.

ARMAND. Then I shall sing to him here. Join me, my friends. Let us sing the song of Jerusalem, the song he loves so well.

SIR DENIS. The king is journeying fast to the Heavenly Jerusalem, Armand. He prays now only for our safe return to France. He calls upon St. James and St. Genevieve, his patrons, to protect his family and his country. But sing your song, my boys. It will cheer us all.

Jerusalem Mirabilis

Translation by S. C.

ANCIENT CRUSADE HYMN

Je-rú-sa-lem mi-rá - bi-lis, Urbs be-á-ti-or ál-i-is,
Je-ru-sa-lem most won - der-ful, Cit-y bless-ed and beau-ti-ful.

Quam pér-ma-nens op-tá - bi-lis — Gau-dén-ti-bus — te An-ge-lis.
Thou art our hope, our last-ing hope — Re-joic-ing all — the an-gel hosts.

PIERRE. Listen. I hear the Miserere. The king is dying. O Sir Denis,
we shall never see the Holy Land.

96

Miserere Mei, Deus

1. Mi-se - ré-re mé-i Dé - us,* se-cún-dum má-gnam mi-se-ri - cór-di-am tú - am.

2. Et secúndum multitúdinem miseratiónum tuárum,* déle iniquitátem méam.

3. Amplius láva me ad iniquitáte méa:* et a peccáto méo múnda me.

4. Quóniam iniquitátem méam ego cognósco:* et peccátum méum contra me est sémper.

English translation:

1. *Have mercy upon me, O God, according to Thy great mercy.*
2. *And according to the multitude of Thy tender mercies, blot out my iniquity.*
3. *Wash me yet more from my iniquity; and cleanse me from my sin.*
4. *For I acknowledge my iniquity, and my sin is always before me.*

SIR DENIS. Pierre, there is a Jerusalem which is above, the Holy City, the Paradise which is our heavenly home. Each of us must journey there, but only those who are pure and just will enter. The king has offered his life to God, pledged his sword to the service of God. He has fought to save the Holy Places from the infidel, and suffered many hardships and much sorrow for the sake of Jerusalem. Now God rewards him, not with the earthly Jerusalem but with the joys of heaven. The king will enter Jerusalem, his royal banner before him, and the angels and the holy martyrs will come to meet him. You and I must travel there too, and God grant we may follow our king into the Heavenly Kingdom, where we shall reign with Christ.

PÈRE CHRISTOPHE (*Entering slowly*). Sir Denis, the king is dead. He died a holy and a happy death.

SIR DENIS. Which may God grant to all of us.

PÈRE CHRISTOPHE. Amen. Come now to the royal tent, all of you, and pray for his soul. (*They all go out, slowly.*)

(As they go out, the Chorus of Holy Martyrs enters and follows Sir Denis, singing "In Paradisum.")

In Paradisum

In pa - ra - dí - sum, de - dú - cant te Án - ge - li: in tú -
Oh, may the an - gels con - duct thee in - to par - a - dise: May the

o ad - vén - tu sus - cí - pi - ant te Már - ty - res, __
ho - ly mar - tyrs re - ceive thee at thy en - trance there. __

et per - dú - cant te in ci - vi - tá - tem sán - ctam Je - rú - sa -
May they lead thy soul in - to the ho - ly cit - y, __ Je - ru - sa -

lem. Chó - rus An - ge - ló - rum te __ sus - cí - pi - at,
lem. May the choirs of an - gels re - ceive thee with joy,

et cum Lá - za - ro quón - dam páu - pe - re ae - tér - nam __
and with La - za - rus who, too, once was poor, may thy soul __

há - be - as __ ré - qui - em.
rest in peace ev - er - more.

98

(*The* CRUSADERS *return, marching slowly, singing "Jerusalem Mira-bilis."*)

Jerusalem Mirabilis

Translation by s. c.

ANCIENT CRUSADE HYMN

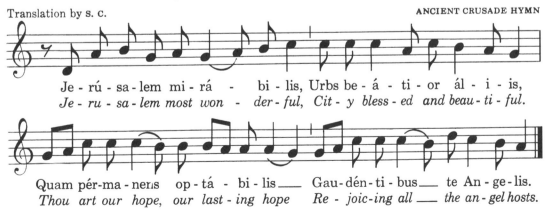

Je - rú - sa - lem mi - rá - bi - lis, Urbs be - á - ti - or ál - i - is,
Je - ru - sa - lem most won - der - ful, Cit - y bless - ed and beau - ti - ful.

Quam pér - ma - nens op - tá - bi - lis___ Gau - dén - ti - bus___ te An - ge - lis.
Thou art our hope, our last - ing hope Re - joic-ing all ___ the an - gel hosts.

THE END

99

We Sing the Mass

Mass XII

Kyrie

Ký - ri - e _____ e - lé - i - son. *iij.*

Chrí - ste _____ e - lé - i - son. *iij.*

Ký - ri - e _____ e - lé - i - son. *ij.*

Ký - ri - e _____ e - lé - i - son.

Gloria

Priest sings: **Choir:**

Gló - ri - a ___ in ex - cél - sis Dé - o. Et in tér - ra pax ho - mí - ni -

bus, bó - nae vo - lun - tá - tis. Lau - dá - mus te. Be - ne - dí - ci - mus te.

100

A-do-rá-mus te. Glo-ri-fi-cá-mus te. Grá-ti-as á-gi-mus ti - bi

pro-pter má-gnam gló-ri - am tú - am. Dó-mi-ne Dé-us, Rex cae-lé-stis,

Dé-us Pá-ter om-ní-po-tens. Dó-mi-ne Fí-li u-ni-gé-ni-te

Jé-su Chrí-ste. Dó-mi-ne Dé - us, A-gnus Dé - i, Fí-li-us Pá-tris.

Qui tól-lis pec-cá-ta mún-di, mi-se-ré - re nó-bis. Qui tól-

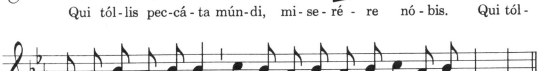

lis pec-cá-ta mún-di, sús-ci-pe de-pre-ca-ti-ó-nem nó-stram.

Qui sé-des ad déx-te-ram Pá-tris, mi-se-ré-re nó-bis.

Quó-ni-am tu só-lus sán-ctus. Tu só-lus Dó-mi-nus. Tu só-lus

Al - tís - si - mus, Jé - su Chrí - ste. Cum Sán-cto Spí - ri - tu

in gló - ri - a Dé - i Pá - tris. A - men. —

Credo 1

Cré - do in ú - num Dé - um, Pá - trem o - mni - po - tén-tem,

fa - ctó-rem caé - li et tér - rae, vi - si - bí - li - um ó - mni - um, —

et — in - vi - si - bí - li - um. Et in ú - num Dó - mi - num —

Jé - sum Chrí - stum, Fí - li - um Dé - i u - ni - gé - ni - tum.

Et ex Pá - tre ná - tum an - te ó - mni - a saé - cu - la. Dé -

um de Dé - o, lú-men de lú - mi - ne,⸺ Dé-um vé-rum de

Dé - o vé - ro. Gé - ni - tum, non fá-ctum, con-sub-stan-ti - á - lem

Pá - tri: per⸺quem ó - mni - a fá - cta sunt. Qui pro-pter nos

hó - mi - nes, et pro-pter nó-stram sa - lú - tem de-scén- dit de cáe - lis.

Et in-car-ná-tus est de Spí - ri - tu Sán-cto ex⸺ Ma - rí -

a Vír - gi - ne: Et⸺hó-mo fá - ctus est. Cru - ci - fí - xus ét-

i - am pro nó - bis: sub Pón - ti - o Pi - lá - to pás - sus, et

se - púl - tus est. Et re-sur - ré - xit tér - ti - a dí - e, se -

cún-dum Scrip-tú-ras. Et a-scén-dit in caé-lum: sé-det

ad déx-te-ram Pá-tris. Et í-te-rum ven-tú-rus est cum gló-ri-

a, ju-di-cá-re vi-vos et mór-tu-os: cú-jus ré-gni

non é-rit fí-nis. Et in Spí-ri-tum Sán-ctum Dó-mi-num,

et vi-vi-fi-cán-tem: qui ex Pá-tre Fi-li-ó-que pro-

cé-dit. Qui cum Pá-tre et Fí-li-o si-mul ad-o-rá-tur,

et con-glo-ri-fi-cá-tur: qui lo-cú-tus est per Pro-phé-tas.

Et ú-nam sán-ctam ca-thó-li-cam et a-po-stó-li-

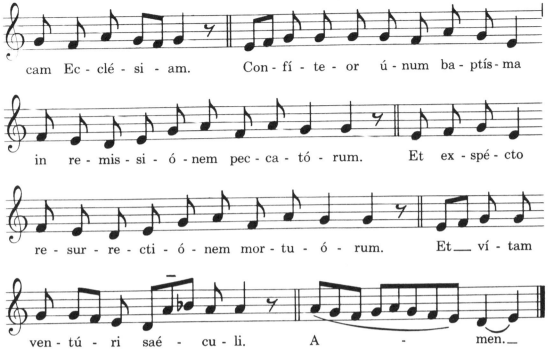

cam Ec - clé - si - am. Con - fí - te - or ú - num ba - ptís - ma

in re - mis - si - ó - nem pec - ca - tó - rum. Et ex - spé - cto

re - sur - re - cti - ó - nem mor - tu - ó - rum. Et__ ví - tam

ven - tú - ri saé - cu - li. A - men.__

Preface

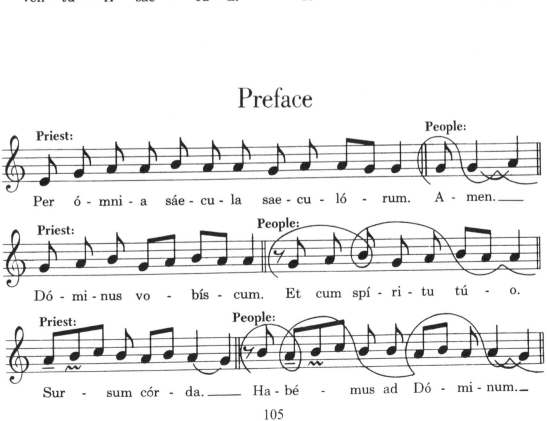

Priest: Per ó - mni - a sáe - cu - la sae - cu - ló - rum. **People:** A - men.__

Priest: Dó - mi - nus vo - bís - cum. **People:** Et cum spí - ri - tu tú - o.

Priest: Sur - sum cór - da.__ **People:** Ha - bé - mus ad Dó - mi - num.__

Priest:

Grá - ti - as _ a - gá - mus Dó - mi - no _ Dé - o nó - stro.

People:

Di - gnum et jús - tum est. _

Sanctus

Sán - ctus, Sán - ctus, Sán - ctus

Dó - mi - nus Dé - us Sá - ba - oth. Plé - ni sunt caé - li et tér - ra

gló - ri - a _ tú - a. Ho - sán - na in ex - cél - sis.

Be - ne - díc - tus qui vé - nit in nó - mi - ne Dó - mi - ni.

Ho - sán - na in ex - cél - sis.

Agnus Dei

A - gnus Dé - i, qui tól - lis pec - cá - ta mún - di: mi - se - ré - re nó - bis. A - gnus Dé - i, qui tól - lis pec - cá - ta mún - di: mi - se - ré - re nó - bis. A - gnus Dé - i, qui tól - lis pec - cá - ta mún - di: dó - na nó - bis pá - cem.

Before the Blessing

Priest: Ite Missa est.
Choir:

Dé - o _____ grá - ti - as

This is one of several ways in which Deo Gratias may be sung.